Theater of War

12/25/05
New York

For Liz and Rodney Berens
Merry Christmas

Theater of War

In Which the Republic Becomes an Empire

◆

LEWIS LAPHAM

[signature]

THE NEW PRESS

Published in the United States by The New Press, New York, 2003
Distributed by W. W. Norton & Company, Inc., New York

ISBN 1-56584-847-0 (pbk.)

Library of Congress Cataloging-in-Publication Data

Lapham, Lewis H.
    Theater of war: in which the republic becomes an empire / Lewis Lapham.
       p.   cm.
    Includes index.
    ISBN 1-56584-772-5 (hc.) ISBN 1-56584-847-0 (pbk.)

    1. United States—Foreign relations—2001-   2. September 11 Terrorist Attacks,
2001.   3. War on Terrorism, 2001-   4. United States—Foreign relations—20th
century.   5. United States—Military policy.   6. National characteristics, American.   7. Messianism, Political—United States.   I. Title.

E902.L37 2002
973.931—dc21

                                                                    2002071889

The New Press was established in 1990 as a not-for-profit alternative to the large,
commercial publishing houses currently dominating the book publishing industry.
The New Press operates in the public interest rather than for private gain, and is
committed to publishing, in innovative ways, works of educational, cultural, and
community value that are often deemed insufficiently profitable.

The New Press, 38 Greene Street, New York, NY 10013
www.thenewpress.com

In the United Kingdom:
6 Salem Road, London W2 4BU

Printed in the United States of America

2   4   6   8   10   9   7   5   3   1

Contents

Introduction

> The gulf between how one should live and how one does live is
> so wide that a man who neglects what is actually done for what
> should be done learns the way to self-destruction rather than
> self-preservation. The fact is that a man who wants to act
> virtuously in every way necessarily comes to grief among
> so many who are not virtuous.
> —NICCOLÒ MACHIAVELLI

*T*he essays in this book take up the story of America's
foreign wars in the near present, during the presidential
election campaign that preceded last year's terrorist
bombings of New York and Washington, D.C., but they depend
for their sense on my recollection of the still not too distant past
in which our enemies were easier to find. Maybe it's a trick of
memory or a sign of age, but when I watch President George W.
Bush threaten a White House television camera with a promise to punish all the world's evildoers, the call to arms sounds
like the sales pitch for an off-road vehicle or a lite beer. I'm old
enough to have heard both Winston Churchill and Franklin D.
Roosevelt address the subjects of war and peace, and I can remember first seeing the United States Navy not as pictures at a

Pentagon press briefing but as ships at anchor in San Francisco Bay.

The Japanese bombed Pearl Harbor in December 1941, the month prior to my seventh birthday, and for the next four years the war to end all wars was seldom out of sight and never out of mind. My grandfather was mayor of the city in 1944, my father serving on the staff of the general forwarding military supplies to the South Pacific; their connections to the headquarters command at Fort Mason allowed my younger brother and myself to some-times go aboard a battleship or a submarine, occasionally to watch the embarkation of an infantry battalion bound for the Marshall Islands, and once (on the flight deck of a badly damaged aircraft carrier) to stand at attention in the presence of Admiral Chester Nimitz. A U.S. Marine colonel came to tell my sixth-grade history class about the landings on Guadalcanal, and a procession of my father's college acquaintances not long in uniform sat drinking gin in the library and saying that they would bring us back a Japanese sword from New Guinea or the Coral Sea. By the time I was eight, I'd learned to draw the silhouette of every kind of plane in the American Air Force, every class of ship in the American Navy; before I was nine I'd committed to memory the roster of American presidents (names, dates in office, distinguishing features, and major accomplishments), and at Christmas dinner in the year I turned ten I stood on a chair in Grandfather's house on Jackson Street to recite the Declaration of Independence.

Victory in Europe in April 1945 was soon followed by the drafting of the United Nations Charter in the San Francisco Opera House; Grandfather delivered the welcoming speech, his face flushed with emotion, his voice vibrant with the promise of a postwar world conceived in the freedom from tyranny and fear. The discussions went on for nine weeks, and because all the members of our family were recruited to entertain the company of visiting diplomats, I can remember passing a tray of puffed cheese to V. M. Molotov, withholding comment on the costume of Saudi Arabia's Prince Faisal, exchanging a remark on the San Francisco fog with John Foster Dulles. Brightened by the joyful waving of a thousand flags, the city overflowed with the feeling that right had conquered wrong, God's will done on earth as it is in Heaven. I believed every word of every speech, in part because I was ten years old, but also, I think in equal part, because many of them were true. They were what the war had been about, their meaning as clear and present as the fleet at anchor in the bay.

America's once certain virtue now seems to me closer to a fiction than a fact, and if the essays in this book run against the tide of much of the commentary published since September 11, 2001, it is because they follow from the premise that the attacks were to be expected and should have come as no surprise. Not because America deserves to be blamed for all the world's misfortune, but because the makers of America's foreign policy over the course of the previous fifty years have embraced a dream of power almost as vainglorious as the one that rallied the disciples of Osama bin Laden to the banner of jihad. For what reason do we possess the largest store of weapons known to the history of mankind if not to kill as many people as we declare to be our enemies? Why then should our enemies not kill us? Taking into account Washington's repeated experiments with the bombing of civilian populations as a form of propaganda meant to sell the splendor of democracy, how does it come to pass that our ranking geopoliticians fail to notice that explosions are hard to copyright? If the logic of globalization allows Chinese bicycle mechanics to manufacture cheap knockoffs of first-run Arnold Schwarzenegger films, what prevents a nonunion crew of Saudi Arabian terrorists from making a low-budget version of the Pentagon's "Operation Enduring Freedom"?

President Bush proposes to answer the questions with never-ending war, and his summons to the flag of holy crusade speaks to the confusions of purpose that have baffled both the authors and critics of American foreign policy for the better part of the last one hundred years. President Teddy Roosevelt's Rough Riders seized the Panama Canal Zone in November 1903 on behalf of what he called "the interests of collective civilization," and in April 1914 President Woodrow Wilson sent several thousand American troops to Mexico to depose a ruler unacceptable to Washington and "to teach the Latin Americans to elect good men."[1] Wilson was a stern moralist who believed himself guided

[1]Both Roosevelt and Wilson conceived of foreign policy as a missionary enterprise; their joint biblical reading of geopolitics set the course of American diplomacy for the whole of the twentieth century. Only once, and then briefly and in passing, did Roosevelt enquire of his attorney general Philander C. Knox about the legal precedent for his seizure of the Canal Zone. "Oh, Mr. President," Knox said, "do not let so great an achievement suffer from any taint of legality." Before invading Mexico in 1914, Wilson put a similar question to Felix Frankfurter, later the Supreme Court Justice but then a young lawyer in what was still known as the War Department. Frankfurter explained that he didn't need to look up any laws. "It's an act of war against a great power," he said. "It's not an act of war against a small power."

by God's will, and when he enlisted the country in the first of the century's world wars, it wasn't entirely clear whether he conceived of America as a religion or a state. His natural form of address was the sermon, and the Fourteen Points that he brought to the Peace Conference in Paris in 1919 were meant to provide the decadent European powers with an equivalent of the secure environment that President Bush now wishes to send to Iran and Iraq, possibly also to Libya, North Korea, Lebanon, Syria, Yemen, and the Philippine archipelago.

A similarly messianic agenda supported the fighting of the Second World War against the Axis powers of Germany, Italy, and Japan as well as the theory of the Cold War against the Russians. Nuclear weapons acquired the powers once assigned to the bones of the saints, and the opaque language of diplomatic compromise was lifted to the pitch of a prophetic crying in the wilderness. For nearly fifty years the military and foreign policy bureaucracies in Washington relied on the evil Soviet empire as the enemy of first resort, as necessary to the American economy as General Motors and Iowa corn, as sure a proof of America's liberties as the Bill of Rights or the fifes and drums in a Fourth of July parade. The constant threat of next week's day of judgment furnished nine American presidents with a just and sacred cause, and the operatic stage set of a world-encircling Communist conspiracy supplied the dark backcloth against which our freedom-loving politicians projected the wholesome images of American innocence and goodness of heart.

The present Bush Administration lacks the old Soviet pedestals on which to stand the statues of America the great, America the good, but its daily press releases talking up the war on terrorism deploy many of the same words that I remember having heard in the San Francisco Opera House in the spring of 1945. When I ask myself why they ring so false, it occurs to me that the increasingly dissolute course of American foreign policy over the past fifty years can best be understood as a rake's progress, the country exhibiting itself in the character of a profligate heir to what was once an immense fortune. The analogy strikes me as apt because America's supremacy following its victories in the Second World War bore the stamp of an inherited estate. Within a matter of six years we acquired, largely by invitation and default, the semblance of an empire, and what was left of Western civilization passed into the American account. Japan was in ruins, and so was Germany; China was in the throes of civil war; France had disintegrated, both as a nation and as the embodiment of an idea; and the British were so sick of their imperial pretensions that they voted Churchill out of office within two months of the German surrender.

During the years between the two world wars the American national interest remained firmly fixed on things American, and if the United States intervened at will in Caribbean or Latin American politics, we did so because the Western Hemisphere so clearly belonged within the sphere of our commercial enterprise that nobody took the trouble to raise the questions of policy with the household servants. Most Americans knew little and thought less about the world beyond the Atlantic and Pacific Oceans; among the privileged classes only a few ornaments of the Ivy League took up careers in the Navy or the State Department. George F. Kennan in his memoirs describes a man who joined the foreign service in order that his mother need not suffer the indignity of a baggage search when passing through customs on her way to Baden-Baden.

The victories over Germany and Japan invested the sons of imperious American matrons with the authority of Roman proconsuls, masters of the narrow earth applauded not only by Belgian shopgirls but also by Japanese militarists and Italian oligarchs, everywhere received by crowds of smiling people who welcomed them with flowers. Being American, we don't draw careful distinctions between different orders of things, and because our best-loved truths hold that God bestows worldly success on those found worthy of His Grace, we accepted our military triumph as clear title to the mandate of Heaven. Fortunately for the lesser nations of the earth, we were American, amiable and good-natured people incapable of doing wrong.

Combine the presumption of limitless virtue with the possession of limitless wealth, and it's only a matter of time before the heir to even the noblest of fortunes comes to imagine that the world is made of painted scenery. The man obliged to earn his own estate learns to make distinctions, knowing that he must study other people's motives and desires if he hopes to gain something from them. Fortune's child doesn't like to bother with details. He never has time to listen to the whole story or to read through the long lists of names that he doesn't know how to pronounce; he has planes to catch and meetings to attend, and so he expects the family lawyers to provide him with gun bearers and conclusions. The habit of mind reduces the complexities of foreign policy to the simplicities of a sporting event—a nation is slave or free, North or South, in the First World or the Third, Communist or Chris-

tian, "with us or against us." The view from the box seats holds
that the embarrassments of death and failure will fall to the lot
of persons to whom one has never been properly introduced.

The rich nation's portfolio of international treaties resembles a
rich man's stock portfolio, stuffed with holdings that he inherited
from his grandfather or his mother's uncles. He has trouble re-
membering the assets and liabilities represented by NATO,
SETO, CENTO, and God knows how many other securities for
which he can't recall the names. The habit of inattention accounts
for his sometimes careless disregard for countries denominated as
allies; because they came with the art collection and the antique
silver they can be sold or deaccessioned when the heir finds himself
pressed for funds with which to stage an extravagant fireworks
display or make a handsome philanthropic gesture. The victories
of 1945 had cost so little in the way of casualties (no damage to
the continental United States, fewer American lives lost than were
lost by the Union army in the Civil War) that the inheritors of
the estate tended to confuse the practice of *realpolitik* with a game
of polo or a play by Bertolt Brecht. African despots can go among
the tribes to instruct them in the magic of constitutional self-
government; alienated poets can be sent to invade Cuba, outfitted
by the CIA with false information, not enough artillery, no aircraft, and the wrong tactics. The rich man applauds, admires the
native handicraft, and sends another gift of weapons.

American presidents get elected because they embody the country's preferred image of itself, and in 1960 John F. Kennedy appeared before the voters as the young Prince Hal riding through

the forest on the road to what *Life* magazine was soon to picture as the cloud-capped tower of Camelot. The media doted on the images of opulent idealism, the handsome dauphin plump with good intentions, willing to "pay any price, bear any burden, meet any hardship, support any friend, oppose any foe" to assure the success of liberty. By January 1961 I'd been assigned as a reporter for the *New York Herald Tribune* to the United Nations building on the East River, and while watching Kennedy's Inaugural Address on a television screen in the delegates' lounge, I nearly came to blows with a correspondent from *Le Monde,* who dismissed the speech as clever sophistry. I told him he was a third-rate fop auditioning for the part of a second-rate cynic. It had been sixteen years since I'd seen the aircraft carriers returning from the victory in the Pacific, but I hadn't forgotten the way that sometimes through the fog under the Golden Gate Bridge they emerged as if from the shadow of death into the sunlight on the bay, and I was still inclined to think that the words of an American president were convertible into the currency of truth.

Not yet having met the Kennedys, I didn't know how quickly it might be possible to squander an inheritance. In New York during what were later known as the Thousand Days between the President's election and his assassination, it was impossible to attend an Upper East Side cocktail party without running across members of the President's supporting cast on their way to Hyannisport for the weekend or to Virginia for a touch-football game. Kennedy made politics fashionable, and by so doing he encouraged the beau monde to look upon his government as a lighthearted entertainment, all the world a theater in which to tell the story of America's enlightened munificence, to stage a revival of liberty in Southeast Asia, improve the character of Guatemala, do something significant for Turkey, effect a change of attitude in the Balkans. The entourage traveling with the presidential house party (noted authors, important movie directors, soon-to-be discovered actresses) seldom made much of a distinction between a morning in Sun Valley for the skiing and an afternoon in Mississippi for an exhibition of black rage.

On the two occasions when I encountered Kennedy in a Fifth Avenue drawing room crowded with his envious followers, I remember being surprised to see a man who seemed as absent as he was present, exhausted by the demands of his distracted sexual appetite. From a distance I'd admired his youthfulness and strength; in the close-up, I thought of a stag brought down by hounds. I don't doubt that Kennedy was a gallant man who aspired to a nobler ideal of the presidency than could be fitted to the media's rubric of "the Kennedy style"; nor do I doubt that he possessed both the courage and the wit attributed to him by the legion of his biographers. Although I do not know it for a fact, I suspect that like many people born to money Kennedy probably found it hard to know the difference between the people who loved him and the people who wanted to kill him. Except in an election year, what difference did it make? Who or what could possibly do him harm? Why not undertake a war in Asia and ride through Dallas in an open car?

Kennedy personified America's postwar supremacy in the character of the spendthrift heir, and I remember first being struck by the likeness soon after the CIA's bungled assault on Cuba's

Bay of Pigs. Joseph Newman, the chief of the *Herald Tribune*'s
U.N. Bureau, was in close touch with the Cuban putsch, and I
can still see two of his informants, both in ill-fitting overcoats,
sitting in the office three days after the invasion had failed, de-
scribing what they regarded as a feckless betrayal. As drawn on a
Washington map overlay by American intelligence officials, the
invasion was a perfect success—a glorious march to Havana ac-
companied by happy peasants in a rejoicing countryside; as carried
out by a band of misguided Cuban exiles under the direction of
CIA officers stupefied by their belief in James Bond novels, the
invasion was a textbook calamity. At precisely the same hour of
the same night that Fidel Castro, dressed in a fatigue uniform and
smoking a cigar, was urging his troops forward into the Zapata
Swamp, Kennedy, dressed in white tie and tails, was dancing at
a White House ball to the tune of "Mr. Wonderful."

About the war in Vietnam (its origins and purpose, the short-
term effects and long-term consequences) enough books have been
written to stock a university library, but even in light of everything else that has been said, I doubt that many people would
dispute the fact that we never knew (or, if knowing, never learned
to explain) what it was we hoped to win. By encouraging the
assassination of Ngo Dinh Diem in Saigon in 1963, the United
States allied itself with a policy of realpolitik no less cynical than
the one against which it supposedly was defending the tree of
liberty. Four American presidents defined the expedition to Southeast Asia as a prolonged covert action and systematically lied to
the American people about the reason for our presence in a country
with which we never declared ourselves at war. As a result of our

effort to rid Indochina of Communism, Vietnam became a unified Communist state; as a result of our effort to teach the world the lessons of democracy, we taught a generation of American citizens to think of their own government as an oriental despotism.

At the beginning, of course, the authors of our policy thought that they could make quick and easy work of the Communist annoyance in a galaxy far, far away. Why not? How could a rabble of underfed peasants resist the will of the greatest military power that ever stalked the earth? The masters of the American century knew that the French had been defeated in Vietnam, that after eight years of bitter fighting they had retired to Europe with casualties of 50,000 dead and 100,000 wounded. Measured in the scale of American optimism and anti-Communist zeal, the facts didn't carry much weight. Nor did the advice of the surviving French officers who said that it was impossible to win a war in Indochina. The French, as President Kennedy later said, were only the French. They lacked the American gift of omnipotence.

Reading the early history of the American engagement in Vietnam (circa 1957–1964) I don't have much trouble finding the analogy to the young prince surrounded by chattering courtiers who hold up pictures and tell him stories—Vietnam a pawn of the godless Russians, "the domino theory" forestalling a Communist invasion on the beaches of Santa Monica, Vietnam the pawn of the wicked Chinese. Almost none of the people in the White House throne rooms knew what they were talking about, but the American foreign policy establishment doesn't place a high priority on a knowledge of history or an acquaintance with languages. It didn't matter that the Vietnamese had been fighting wars for 2,000 years against the Chinese and the Mongols, as well as against the Japanese and the French. Nor did it matter that Ho Chi Minh's politics were local and expedient, in no way connected to a global conspiracy; Ho was a Communist and therefore allied with the Antichrist. Seized with the fervor of ideological crusade, American statesmen at the time found it easy to imagine Communists lurking like trolls in all the world's forests, and they didn't draw careful distinctions between a Soviet tank in Poland, a conversation about Karl Marx in a Paris café, or a national independence movement in Hanoi. Nor did we allow the facts to cloud our picture of Diem as an enlightened democrat constitutionally elected to govern a free and independent nation treacherously attacked by a foreign enemy across an international frontier. None of the catalogue copy was true. South Vietnam was a synthetic state manufactured in Washington, D.C., subject to the whim of American policy and money, embroiled in civil war, ruled by a succession of second-rate despots unable to command the loyalty or affection of the Vietnamese people.

Relying on a similar set of false premises, the American generals directing the war that wasn't a war substituted cheerful summaries of fictitious success for the unsightly data of defeat. They conceived of Vietnam as a factory that accepted the living flesh of the enemy as raw material to be processed into the commodity of victory. American soldiers were carried on the books as costs of production, like soap or radios or boxes of ammunition; their commanders spoke of body counts, kill ratios, targets of high-yield opportunity. What was real was the dehumanized image of war that appeared on the flowcharts and the computer screens. What was not real was the human experience of pain, suffering, mutilation, and death.

Prior to the defeat in Vietnam, most Americans didn't question their credentials as honorable people unerringly drawn to the side of what was right and true; not the kind of people who slaughtered 100,000 Cambodian peasants on Christmas Eve or pushed their houseboys off the last helicopter out of Saigon. The war proved them mistaken in this judgment, but nobody in Washington stood willing to say why the country had betrayed its own dearest principles, or how it had come to pass that so many of its best college students were staging street protests and burning the American flag. Instead of acknowledging its cherished stupidity and arrogance, the government blamed the news media for writing the wrong stories and taking the wrong pictures. The accusation was as ignorant as it was unfair; for almost ten years the news media had refrained from doubting the justice of the American presence in Indochina, but by 1968 a few of their more observant operatives couldn't help but take note of the official lies so often and so badly told, and the prime-time sequence of brutal images— a straw village set afire with a soldier's cigarette lighter, a Vietcong prisoner summarily executed by a pistol shot to the head, a little girl, naked on a road, smeared with the light of burning napalm—forced the American television audience to bear witness to the killing done in its name.

It was not a sight that sold hair products or won elections, and the makers of American foreign policy, nurtured in the paranoid atmospheres of the Cold War, found it convenient to borrow from their Communist enemies the habit of lying to their own citizens on behalf of what they defined as "the national security." Troubled officials sometimes referred to what they called the "paradox" implicit in the waging of secret war under the jurisdiction of a supposedly free, open, and democratic society; their embarrassment didn't prevent a succession of American presidents from entrusting their dreams of omnipotence to the care of apprentice Bismarcks assembled in the White House basement.[2]

On taking office as President in 1969, Richard Nixon immediately equipped his National Security Council with the de facto and de jure authority to make foreign policy without reference to either the Congress or the Constitution, and although most of the time he knew whose telephones to tap, on the larger questions of policy he was almost always wrong. He thought the United States could win the Vietnam War if only the Air Force dropped another twelve tons of explosives on another four rice paddies; he miscal-

---

[2]On arrival in office, every newly elected President finds his grand geopolitical strategies thwarted by Washington's permanent government—the Congress, the news media, the civil and military bureaucracies that bring up the niggling reasons why the schemes can't possibly succeed. Frustrated by the checks and balances of a democratic republic, the President turns to his own provisional government—the band of freebooting ideologues that traveled with him on the road to the White House. The parvenu statesmen possess the talents and energies useful to the winning of elections, which, although sometimes admirable, don't have much bearing on the intricacies of international relations. Eager to take bold stands and launch new initiatives (i.e., to make good on the candidate's fatuous campaign rhetoric), the President's men decide that it's best to make policy in secret, "to take it inside" or "move it across the street"; they start speaking in code, and before long things begin to go very wrong in Guatemala or East Timor or Beirut.

culated the result of the bombing and invasion of Cambodia—the North Vietnamese "sanctuaries" that he meant to destroy didn't exist—and he didn't foresee the economic consequences of the separation of the American dollar from the gold standard. Consistently ignoring intelligence reports that didn't confirm his own theories and suspicions, he was wrong about the Arabian oil cartel and the nature of the Communist conspiracy; most of his attempts at realpolitik ended in failure, and at the end he was even wrong about the character of the American people, misjudging their response to his complicity in the Watergate burglaries.

It's true that Nixon pursued the opening to China, which, given the circumstances, was a feat of diplomacy comparable to conceding the existence of the Pacific Ocean, but very little evidence in the record of his presidency supports his pretensions to statesmanship. A close reading of the small print suggests that he could be relied upon to break any promise, deny any principle, betray any ally or nominal friend. His hatred of free speech was apparent in his every gesture and expression; believing himself destined to rule by decree and interoffice memorandum, he was forever scribbling furious imperatives in the margins of the daily press summaries, instructing his courtiers to rid him of his enemies both real and imagined. The transcripts of Nixon's White House tapes show his verbs to be always violent—"Get someone to hit him!" "Fire him!" "Freeze him!" "Cut him!" "Knock him down!" "Bomb them!" Of his own character he entertained such overblown evaluations that prior to his first meeting with the Russian premier Leonid Brezhnev in the spring of 1972, he directed Henry Kissinger, who preceded him to Moscow, to announce him as a man who was "direct, honest, strong." He was, in fact, devious, dishonest, and weak, a sly and cunning man constantly preparing the photo-op of his place in history. On the eve of another of his departures for Moscow Nixon compared himself to both William the Conqueror en route to the Battle of Hastings and Dwight Eisenhower on the morning of D-Day.[3]

If the years between 1960 and 1968 established the thesis of the 1960s (Camelot), the years from 1968 to 1974 developed the antithesis (Watergate), and just as Kennedy embodied the persona of the American state as luminous romance, Nixon embodied the persona of the American state as grotesque melodrama. Before

---

[3]The standard iconographies routinely mention Nixon's "brilliant" intellect and "enigmatic" character. Neither adjective is easy to align with the noun. Kissinger, Nixon's national security adviser, liked to make fun of his patron's "meatball mind" (i.e., another of the dissolute heirs to the American geopolitical estate), and he often telephoned his more sardonic confederates to read aloud from the President's memoranda, laughing at the pomposity of the language and the threadbare emptiness of the thought. Nixon's several books extend and annotate the joke. The writing is poor, the arguments trite, the author's voice as sententious as that of a latter-day Polonius. Fond of belaboring the obvious, Nixon never fails to inform his readers that the Russians cannot be trusted, that a surprising number of people exist in a state of poverty, and that war isn't a game of Parcheesi.

On one of the tape recordings impounded by the Watergate investigation, he speaks to Chuck Colson about the great task of chastising the legion of his enemies in a voice hard to reconcile with the image of the benevolent sage: "One day we will get them . . . get them on the floor and step on them, crush them, show no mercy. And we'll stick our heels in, step on them hard and twist . . . right, Chuck, right?"

1968 most politicians were presumed trustworthy until proven guilty of fraud or discovered with a striptease dancer in a Baltimore hotel. Maybe not all of them were as handsome as Jack Kennedy on the deck of a yacht, or Jimmy Stewart in the movie *Mr. Smith Goes to Washington;* quite possibly most of them couldn't qualify as Eagle Scouts, but they were thought to know the difference between the public interest and their own. After 1968 it was assumed that any Mr. Smith who went to Washington brought with him the modus operandi of a racetrack tout and the morals of a stoat. The fashionable celebration of government became the equally fashionable abuse of government, and the collective rapture of the Peace Corps gave way to the collective rapture of a race riot in Detroit. It's been nearly thirty years since Nixon was frog-marched out of the White House in August 1974, but the single word "Watergate" still brings to mind not only the burglaries at the building of that name but also the subsequent impeachment proceedings in Congress, the assassinations of Robert Kennedy and Martin Luther King Jr., Henry Kissinger's portentous voice mixed with the sound of incoming artillery at Danang, clouds of tear gas drifting across college lawns and the steps of the Pentagon.

The spasm of guilt and recrimination that followed the Watergate inquiries made possible Jimmy Carter's election to the White House in 1976. A twice-born Christian known for his habit of teaching Sunday school Bible classes, Carter traveled the political circuit in the persona of the innocent American farmer, barefoot and without guile, in search of "a government as good as its people." He promised to redeem the country, not to govern it, and he told his audiences how he was "an eager student" doing his best to learn "all those complicated things that the folks talked about up there in Washington, D.C.," of how it wasn't the American people who had decided to do all those "dreadful things" in Vietnam, Cambodia, Chile, and the West Wing of the White House, of "the deep yearning for intimacy" he'd discovered out there "in this great country of ours."

To the discussion of America's diplomatic affairs Carter brought revelations instead of policies, envisioning a Palestinian state risen in the mist somewhere near the Sea of Galilee, informing a lobbyist from Boeing that he had decided against the deployment of the B-1 bomber because he had asked God about it, and God had told him that that the bomber could do nothing but harm, offering a New Year's toast in Teheran on the last night of 1977 to "America's great friend and ally" Iran, an "island of stability" in the Middle East. A year later Iran was in the midst of revolution and Washington was advising the Shah to abdicate in favor of any government, civil or military, that could restore production in the southern oil fields.

The American electorate doesn't require its presidential candidates to know where to look on the map for Zanzibar or Romania. The lack of knowledge on the topics of foreign affairs is a proof of virtue. The man that would be president must present himself as an innocent and clean-limbed fellow, who knows nothing of ambition, murder, cowardice, or lust, and why would such a true American have taken the trouble to learn a lot of foreign names? The president's ignorance remands the making of the country's foreign policy to a cadre of privy counselors recruited from the

membership of the Council on Foreign Relations—lawyers, bankers, corporation executives who define the public interest as the
freight forwarding agent for their own private interests.[4] Because
the doctrine of American exceptionalism forbids an American
president to notice any contradiction between what he says and
what he does, the family retainers perform the service of doing
things in the heir's name but not in his sight. In this respect they
resemble New York divorce lawyers, who, for the sake of the children, find it prudent to blackmail the showgirl wife with photographs of her debut in a New Orleans brothel. During periods of
relative optimism and extravagance, the family retainers permit
the indulgence of a youthful folly (Kennedy allowed to play with
the toy of political assassination in Cuba and the Congo); in periods of sober reassessment they advise against doing anything that
might injure either the integrity of the trust fund or their own
balance sheets (Carter encouraged after the debacle in Iran to curry
favor with any nation, slave or free, willing to guarantee the safety
of the oil price).

   During the early months of Carter's tenure in the White House

---

[4]To list the names of the prominent secretaries of state or defense over the previous fifty years (Dean Rusk, Robert McNamara, McGeorge Bundy, Henry Kissinger, Harold Brown, James Schlesinger, Caspar Weinberger, George Shultz,
Warren Christopher, Dick Cheney, Donald Rumsfeld, etc., etc.) is to list not
only the members of the Council on Foreign Relations but also those of the
country's better golf clubs—stalwart oligarchs, firm in their loyalty to the mon-
ied interest, sound in their distrust of the moral or political imagination, apt to
believe that nobody is fully human unless he or she possesses an income of at
least $1 million a year.

the American television audience chose to believe that his spiritualization of politics conferred a blessing upon the Republic, that the rituals of atonement took precedence over the secular and more difficult business of providing people with jobs, housing, money, hope, and law. The mood of repentance was short-lived. By the winter of 1978 the majority opinion had tired of the President's sermons about the sadness of the national "malaise." Carter continued to struggle up and down the hills of Maryland wearing his jogger's sweatband as if it were a crown of thorns, but the mortification of his twice-born flesh inspired as little enthusiasm among the American electorate as did Christ's arrival among the populace in Jerusalem riding the foal of an ass instead of a horse, armed not with a sword but with the lamp of faith. In the election of 1980 the voters turned away from Carter as if from a coroner's report, choosing to embrace their new savior in the person of Ronald Reagan, who also promised to restore America to a state of spiritual and temporal grace but who did so with the offer to substitute happy problems for sad problems because, as his wife explained to a reporter during the last week of the campaign, "Ronald really hates to have conflict around him. He doesn't want to have to get on the plane having to hold his stomach."

Elected in what the media promoted as a "landslide," Reagan conceived the American presidency as the starring role in a major motion picture directed by Cecil B. DeMille, and during the whole of his eight years in the White House he always knew precisely where to stand, hitting his marks, tipping his cap. Flawless in his impersonations of both John Wayne and Gene Kelly. Reagan exemplified the spirit of an age of mock heroic empire, and his album of golden commonplaces conformed to the standards of moral and intellectual insignificance that had become synonymous with the art of politics among people who no longer expected their presidents to argue a coherent system of thought or to bring to office anything other than an amateur's best guess about the mysteries of government. The Saturday matinee audience understood that Reagan's political ideas didn't matter as much as his instincts, his prejudices, and his sentiments.[5] Here at last was an accommodating man at ease in the haze of gossip and the company of scoundrels, whose best hope for the nation he expressed in his assurance that the United States will "above all" continue to be a country "where someone could always get rich."

The Reagan Administration's foreign policy played as vaudeville, but the President seemed to have such a good time on the stage of office that it was easy not only to forgive him his frequent lapses of memory (the name of the Soviet prime minister; the whereabouts of Poland) but also to overlook the clownishness of his privy counselors (among them General Danny Graham and CIA director William Casey), who discovered their theories of geopolitics in the novels of Tom Clancy and Louis L'Amour. The games of imperial "Let's Pretend" culminated in

[5]Reagan cried when he first saw the television commercials announcing that it was "morning in America." Riding in a limousine to his first economic summit conference in 1983, he was asked by James Baker, then secretary of the treasury, if he had read the briefing book. Reagan looked at Baker with an expression of genuine bewilderment and concern, as if he had been asked a question to which all right-thinking people already knew the answer. "But, Jim," he said, "*The Sound of Music* was on last night."

the Iran-Contra arms deal, which carried the White House opera troupe into a comic farce with a consortium of Middle Eastern thugs, sharpers, bankrupts, arms smugglers, cutthroats, swindlers, and disbanded soldiers. The plot followed the lines of an episode of *The A-Team,* and on being discovered in their criminal charades, all present conducted themselves in the manner traditional among thieves: everybody professed his own innocence and assigned the fault to a friend. Secretary of State George Shultz and Vice President George Bush moved fastidiously upwind from any prior knowledge, and those who could do so, among them Lieutenant Colonel Oliver North, offered to incriminate one or more of their companions in return for safe passage into the nearest book deal. Whatever they thought they were doing—in Iran, Switzerland, Israel, Nicaragua, Brunei, and the Arabian Peninsula—probably never will be fully understood or explained. Nobody could say with any degree of certainty what had happened to the money, the hostages, the weapons, or the President's senses. Seeking to explain the confusion in his memoirs, *An American Life,* Reagan fell back among the cushions of wistful regret:

> On the day that John Poindexter came to the Oval Office to resign, I didn't ask him the questions I now wish I had. If we hadn't acted so quickly, maybe he and North would have told me some of the things that are still a mystery to me after all this time.
>
> If I could do it over again, I would bring both of them into the Oval Office and say, "Okay, John and Ollie, level

with me. Tell me what really happened and what it is that you have been hiding from me. Tell me everything."

If I had done that, at least I wouldn't be sitting here, writing this book, still ignorant of some of the things that went on during the Iran-Contra affair.

The President's ignorance did him no harm. Actors get hired to read scripts, and by the time Reagan moved into the White House in the winter of 1981 America's military commanders had come to understand that they were in the communications business, not in the business of waging war. The defeat of our armies in Vietnam had forced the Pentagon to the discovery that American soldiers were too precious to dispatch to what it designated as "nonpermissive environments," and the sophistication of the electronic gadgetry made it possible to present colorful explosions in picturesque locations as public service announcements about the enduring values of Western civilization. The new strategy transformed the old practice of gunboat diplomacy into a program of gunboat philanthropy. The eighteenth- and nineteenth-century colonial powers usually had a prize in view—gold, slaves, bananas, the rescue of the British consul, the amputation of an insolent pasha's right hand. The improved technologies blurred the distinction between the reasons of state and the uses of publicity, and the actor president could preach the sermons of holy crusade against all the world's evildoers safe in the Christian assurance that it was better to give than to receive.

Reagan conducted the first successful demonstration of the new postmodern diplomacy off the coast of Libya in August 1981. He wished to "make American power impressive to the enemies of freedom," to set an example not so much before the Libyans (already deemed Barbary pirates) as before the Cubans, the Soviets, the Europeans, the Africans, and any of his own countrymen still troubled by the American defeat in Vietnam. The Libyans had been harassing American aircraft for several years, and the President knew that he could count upon them to continue the practice if the U.S. Navy sailed into the heathen Gulf of Sidra. Naval intelligence had vouched for the inferiority of the Libyan Air Force—an eminently safe enemy, sufficiently villainous to deserve the wrath of eagles but sufficiently weak to guarantee the prospect of no resistance.

The Libyan dictator Muammar Khadafy was happy to serve as coproducer of the performance. Libya also had suffered reverses in recent years, and within the Arab spheres of influence the colonel had few friends and an unfortunate reputation as a zealous employer of assassins. He needed to restore his image as an innocent victim of American imperialism, and here was a chance sent by a merciful Allah to remind the faithful that The Great Satan had come to darken an Arab shore. His pilots had to make at least forty-five passes at the American F-14s before two of them managed to get shot down; the combat lasted roughly sixty seconds, avoided the loss of a single life, and destroyed military property valued at less than one day's expenditure for the forty-three private armies then campaigning in Lebanon. For so small a cost, how large and dramatic an effect. By means of prime-time imagery, Reagan and Khadafy succeeded in arranging what in the old diplomatic parlance used to be described as "a full and frank exchange of views." Their joint production of "Thirty Seconds Over Libya" established the precedent not only for the subsequent invasion of Grenada but also for the tactic of fitting displays of military prowess to the schedule and requirements of network television.

God was still an important character in the movie, of course, and Reagan knew that when calling upon His assistance to thwart the wicked Russians it was always best to gaze upward at a cloud. I don't know whether he believed that God existed somewhere other than on the Warner Brothers set; some of his biographers claim that he kept track of the approaching Rapture, others that he expected to be among the dignitaries invited to the Second Coming of Christ. It's conceivable that his faith was genuine, at least to the point of his being certain that God was an American who looked like a somewhat older Charlton Heston, but I don't think he carried the crusader's cross very far beyond the frontier of heartfelt sentiment. He was an actor who knew that he was an actor, and if God had been part of the story of America's triumph in the world for as long as anybody could remember, who was Ronald Reagan to meddle with the dialogue.

The President's foreign policy advisers liked to present themselves in the character of hard-eyed geopoliticians wise in the ways of empire, willing to send thousands to their deaths in pursuit of the national interest, but the more often I listened to them talk, the more I was inclined to think of them as movie critics. For the most part they worried about the sending of signals, about the transfer of symbols and "America's credibility in the world," and by the middle 1980s the conversation sometimes could get pretty refined. At dinner one night in Washington I came across a government official saying of Nicaragua that he was depressed by "the quality of the regime." Judging only by the tone of his voice, it would have been possible to assume that he was talking about a second-rate wine or a Hyatt Hotel gone to seed at a beach resort no longer attractive to the sponsors of golf tournaments. He wasn't concerned about Nicaragua's capacity to harm the United States; the army was small and ill-equipped, the mineral assets not worth the cost of a first-class embassy. Nor did the official think the governing junta particularly adept at exporting "the virus of Marxist revolution." What troubled him was the "indecorousness of the regime." Nicaragua was in bad taste.

The first President Bush didn't possess Reagan's ear for the perfectly balanced cliché, but he understood the art of imperial moviemaking, and he mounted the invasion of Panama in December 1989 as a tribute to the country's storied military history— parachute drops in the manner of World War II, helicopter gunships suggestive of Vietnam, a million-dollar bounty on the head of a bandit escaped from a tale of the Old American West. Two years later, when introducing his theory of a "new world order" in conjunction with the raid on the Persian Gulf, Bush joined Reagan's dramaturgy with Woodrow Wilson's cherished doctrine of "Peace Without Victory." He had it in mind to prove to the lesser nations of the earth that any misbehavior on their part (any sacking of cities or setting of commodity prices without permission from Washington) would be promptly and severely punished. Never, he said, would Saddam Hussein be able to receive any reward, honor, acclaim, or benefit for his trespass in the desert.

No sir, under no circumstances, not while the United States still had bombs to send eastward out of Eden. The President's right-eousness waxed increasingly militant as the merely secular arguments in favor of the war (the ones about the price of oil, the preservation of American jobs and the American way of life) failed to drum up a cheering crowd. Shifting his flag to the higher ground of the spiritual imperative, Bush redefined the eighteenth-century balance of power as the twelfth-century peace of God. The old Cold War doctrine of containment had bound the United States to pro-tect the world only from Communists; the new doctrines of aggres-sive humanitarianism not only broadened and extended the mission but also guaranteed the safety of the defense budget. Unlike the lost Soviet empire, the kingdom of Hell could be relied upon never to go bankrupt or abandon the war for the soul of mankind.

The transformation of the American military establishment into an order of blameless monks fit President Bill Clinton's agenda as the man from Hope. Speaking to the American Society of News-paper Editors in the spring of 1999, Clinton explained the new season's admonishment of the Balkans as a skirmish in "the great battle" between "the forces of globalism and the forces of tribal-ism." Like his immediate predecessors in the White House, Clin-ton understood foreign policy as a Hollywood action picture, and he followed Reagan's "Sands of Grenada" and Bush's "Dark Moon Over Baghdad" with "Goodbye to Belgrade." Slobodan Milosevic declined the invitation to attend the awards ceremonies, but at least he knew how to set up the location shots and the crowd scenes. Operation Allied Force paid for the special effects; Milo-sevic's police supplied intimate close-ups of human misery on the

Albanian frontier. No soldiers at risk on either soundstage, each of the coproducers free to advertise their politics as a popular detergent (Milosevic's ethnic cleansing, NATO's moral cleansing), cameo roles for the Russians and Vanessa Redgrave as well as for Jesse Jackson and the president of France.

Severe in manner and terse in speech, the military spokesmen appeared at a podium every night in Brussels or Washington to say that the NATO aircraft had enjoyed another wonderful day of bombing in Yugoslavia. They displayed maps and video-highlight reels, listed targets, counted sorties, apologized for occasional technical errors (the odd cruise missile wandering off into Bulgaria or finding a hospital instead of a bridge), reaffirmed their faith in democracy, and said that the tyrant must not be allowed to continue his massacre of the innocents. A little later in the program the camera angles shifted to the mountains of Macedonia, where sympathetic news correspondents culled the herd of refugees for those among them who had brought prize-winning stories to tell. Here was Bajram, whose three sons had been beheaded, and there was Shala, who had been raped by fourteen Serbian soldiers in Pec, and over here, just behind the tractor, we have little Besim, age nine, who watched his father and mother being burned to death in a barn.

What was difficult to understand was the lack of connection between the two sets of images, the absence of cause and effect. To hear the gentlemen in Washington and Brussels talk about the avowed purpose of Operation Allied Force (to stop the killing in Kosovo), one might have expected to see some sort of military maneuver in the southern Balkans—possibly a few helicopters or the arrival of an armored vehicle. But Kosovo, alas, was "a non-permissive environment," too dangerous for allied soldiers (who might come up against mortars or machine guns), too dangerous for low-flying helicopters (which might encounter handheld rockets), too dangerous for the briefing officers with the video-highlight reels (who might find themselves at a loss for an overhead projector and a sufficient number of leather chairs). And so NATO attacked Belgrade. Like the Gulf of Sidra, Panama, and the Iraqi desert, Belgrade wasn't dangerous. The planes could come and go at will, dropping their bombs like sermons from the superior altitudes of moral certainty, leaving it to the tyrant Milosevic to draw the correct analogy between a pulpit and a B-52.

If Reagan was an actor playing a politician, Clinton was a politician playing an actor. Both product and personification of the celebrity culture, Clinton, like Carter, hadn't been elected to govern the country. In 1992 and 1996 the country was being run (and run very nicely, thank you) by the corporations, the media syndicates, and Alan Greenspan. The voters in both election years chose the candidate most likely to tell them stories—amusing and heartwarming stories about the prosperous economy and the digital American future; scandalous stories about the murder of Vincent Foster, drug dealers rafting on the Whitewater River, Gennifer Flowers in her cheerleader outfit, Susan McDougal in chains. In a world arranged to the satisfaction of the Disney company and the bond market, what was the White House if not a movie set, and who was the President of the United States if not a carnival king?

The younger President Bush seems to think the movie is real, and when he stood before the White House microphones on the morning of March 11 to commemorate the passage of six months since the attacks on Washington and New York, it wasn't hard to guess that he had come to renew his summons to the banners of medieval crusade. Addressing 1,300 dignitaries assembled on the South Lawn (Supreme Court justices, members of Congress, cabinet ministers, senior military officers, the Washington diplomatic corps), the President wished to assure the faithful that their cause was just, their enemies everywhere discomfited or targeted for destruction. Sensitive to the ecumenical character of his audience (Muslims and some Buddhists as well as Christians in the crowd), the President was careful to make only one reference to the God of Abraham and Pat Robertson. He phrased his message in the vernacular—"terrorists" instead of "all the world's evildoers," the "mighty coalition of civilization" instead of "the Bride of the Lamb"—but it was apparent from the evangelical certainty in his voice that he was talking about the armies of light come against the legions of darkness on the field of Armageddon.

If the words weren't those of the church militant, their meaning was as plain as the crusader's cross blessed by Urban II on the meadow of Clermont in the year of our Lord 1095. A tall man robed in white, the pontiff spoke with "sweet and persuasive eloquence," and as reconstituted by Evan S. Connell in *Deus lo Volt! Chronicle of the Crusades,* the words have weathered the wreck of time:

> "We hear ominous tidings. We hear of a malevolent race, withdrawn from the communion of our belief, Turks, Per-

32   THEATER OF WAR

sians, Arabs, accursed, estranged from God, that have laid
waste by fire and sword to the walls of Constantinople, to
the Arm of St. George. . . . Turks perforate the navels of
God's servants, pull forth and bind their intestines to stakes,
lead them about while viscera discolor the earth. They pierce
Christians with arrows, flog the suffering. What else can we
say? What more shall be said? To whom, therefore, does the
task of vengeance fall, if not to you?"

In place of Urban's eloquence, President Bush offered money
and guns to any nation willing to rally to the oriflamme of Christ
(not among the 179 sovereign flags present on the lawn but the
one under which the others could expect to serve), and when he
reached his peroration—"I see a peaceful world beyond the war
on terror . . . may God bless our coalition"—I was reminded not
only of Wilson's moral commandments but also of the President's
father, standing at the same White House microphones in December 1992, dispatching American troops to Somalia with a prelate's
benediction: "And so, to every sailor, soldier, airman, and marine
who is involved in this mission, let me say we are doing God's
work. We will not fail. Thank you, and may God bless the United
States of America."[6]

[6]By making the conduct of foreign policy a matter of conscience—subject to the
emotional weight and force of the film footage as well as to the number of
available tanks—the rulers of the state come to imagine that the expressions of
their private feelings serve as statements of public policy, and foreign military
intervention becomes a drama in the theater of the self. A week before the first
President Bush announced his decision to rescue Somalia in the winter of 1992,

The second President Bush also announces himself as a doer of God's work, but it's hard to judge the degree of his trust in Holy Scripture. The few indications available in the press suggest the temperament of a true believer—a born-again Christian who as governor of Texas named June 20 as "The Day of Jesus"; a moralizing politician fond of drawing the line in the sand between Good and Evil. If a man's qualities can be inferred from what is known about the company he keeps, then Bush's appointment of John Ashcroft to the office of the attorney general doesn't speak well for his ability to separate the powers of the church from the powers of the state.

Ashcroft makes no secret of his righteousness or his conception of the Justice Department as an agent of divine retribution. Since the American declaration of war on terrorism the attorney general has been quick to order mass arrests, suspend the right to habeas corpus, deny requests forwarded to the government under the Freedom of Information Act, draw up legislation equipping his office with the authority to tap anybody's telephone and open everybody's mail. When questioned by the Senate Judiciary Committee last December about the Pentagon's scheme to bring suspected terrorists secretly to trial before a military tribunal,

---

the White House press corps found him moody and out of sorts, depressed about the loss of the election and complaining, only partly in jest, that he had nothing left to do except walk the dogs. His privy counselors apparently recommended the Somalian adventure as a means of raising his spirits. So also President Clinton in August 1998; three days after testifying about his penis before a Washington grand jury, he revenged himself against the stain on Monica Lewinsky's blue dress by sending cruise missiles into Afghanistan and the Sudan.

Ashcroft all but accused his examiners of treason—"To those who scare peace-loving people with phantoms of lost liberty, my message is this: your tactics only aid terrorists, for they erode national unity and diminish our resolve."

When not otherwise occupied with the zealous search for terrorists and traitors, Ashcroft presides over the Justice Department in the manner of a pastor administering a church. He begins the day at 8:00 A.M. sharp with a meeting devoted to Bible study and a joining of hands in prayer. Sometimes he sings uplifting songs of his own composition in the sentimental baritone of a 1950s Las Vegas lounge singer; occasionally he distributes copies of the sheet music and invites the government officials in the room to sing along.[7]

Having read Ashcroft's speeches and watched him testify before Congress, I don't know where to find much difference between his messianic faith and the similarly fervent sense of spiritual certainty said to comfort the disciples of jihad. Three years ago in Greenville, South Carolina, Ashcroft informed the graduating class at

---

[7]A representative lyric:

> *Let the eagle soar,*
> *Like she's never soared before.*
> *From rocky coast to golden shore,*
> *Let the mighty eagle soar.*
>
> *Soar with healing in her wings,*
> *As the land beneath her sings:*
> *"Only God, no other kings."*

Bob Jones University that in America "we have no king but Jesus"; speaking to 6,000 religious broadcasters last February in Nashville, Tennessee, he reconfirmed the statement, explaining that our American freedoms come to us from Heaven, "not the grant of any government or document, but our endowment from God." The congregation seconded the motion with a steady murmuring of amens; many bowed their heads in prayer. The followers of Osama bin Laden believe that they act in accordance with the instruction of Allah. The attorney general of the United States apparently believes that God wrote the U.S. Constitution and the Bill of Rights. Among the lesser but equally misplaced truth that Ashcroft in his autobiography, *On My Honor,* credits for having given shape and meaning to his life, he lists as ninth on a roster of twenty his discovery that "the verdict of history is inconsequential; the verdict of eternity is what counts." The dogma nullifies the premise on which the United States was founded—a government of laws made by men, for and with other men, framed to the contingencies of the world in time and subject to no other verdict except that of history—but I don't doubt that Ashcroft's view enjoys broad support among pilots trained to fly heavy airplanes into their appointments with destiny.

To what extent Ashcroft's piety reflects the thinking of other officials in the upper echelons of government I have no way of knowing. On the President's cabinet ministers and close advisers the White House praetorians impose a rule of silence not unlike the Mafia's code of *omertà.* But from what I can see and hear in the news media of the administration's more visible apologists (fierce newspaper columnists as well as socioeconomic theorists,

conservative and neoconservative members of Congress), the bulk
of the prevailing jingoism leans heavily toward the ideology of
Holy Crusade. The country's warmaking powers serve at the pleasure of people who seem more sympathetic to the religious enthusiasms of John Ashcroft than to the secular concerns of the
United Nations—a synod of moralists quick to issue writs of cen-
sure and to add another 40,000 names to the list of the world's
evildoers.

The Bush Administration asks to be judged not on the proofs
of what it says and does but on the assertions of its purity of
heart. Convinced that it knows what's best and suspicious of any
advice or consent issuing from the Congress, the White House
regards questions about the war in progress—Where else do we
mean to send the troops? How will we know if and when we've
won?—as divisive and unpatriotic. Thus, with little or no debate, the government over the past six months has withdrawn
from the 1972 ABM Treaty, deployed special operations forces
in at least six foreign countries, and steadily enlarged the drop
zone of its vengeance—the person of Osama bin Laden becoming Al Qaeda headquarters in Afghanistan, then the government
that "harbored" those headquarters, then all other countries that
"harbor" or "sponsor" terrorists unaffiliated with the bombings
of September 11.

Meanwhile, of course, the prayer group in Washington has been
busy with the work of adding to the capacity of America's own
nuclear arsenal. On March 10, the day before President Bush
stepped forward to the White House microphones in the persona
of an eleventh-century pope, the newspapers published a summary

of the Pentagon's newly revised "Nuclear Posture Review," a document apparently leaked to a reporter by a military officer who had reasons to be nervous. The operative paragraphs mentioned the need for "more flexible nuclear strike capabilities," for "more options" with which to confront contingencies "immediate, potential and unexpected," for warheads that penetrate "deep bunkers" in which heathen outlaws might try to escape the wrath of Heaven, for improved intelligence and better targeting systems, for a doctrine of preemptive nuclear attack, allowing the United States to threaten any country that disturbs the peace of God: the Iraqis if they attack Israel, the North Koreans if they attack the South Koreans, the Chinese if they attempt the acquisition of Taiwan.

It so happened that I read the Pentagon policy statement on the same day that I watched the President hearten the multitude on the White House lawn. Listening to him say that "Every nation should know that, for America, the war on terror is not just a policy, it's a pledge," I wondered whether his speechwriters had cribbed the line from an old Ronald Reagan movie or from one of Woodrow Wilson's sermons.

First published in *Harper's Magazine* between October 2000 and June 2003, the essays in this book pick up the thread of the American narrative at the turn of a new millennium and argue for the proposition that maybe the time has come to drop the pose of innocence, kick the habit of entitlement, and write God out of the movie script. Unless we take all three precautions, I don't know how we prevent our democratic enterprise from collapsing into the ruin of its carelessness and good intentions.

During the second half of the twentieth century, generally acknowledged as America's own, fortune's child could buy the world's friendship at the market price, or court its favor by the setting of high-minded examples and the promulgation of lofty sentiment. Statesmen of generous impulse brought forth the Marshall Plan and the Peace Corps, also the instruments of public policy and private charity through which we distributed bread and circuses to every quadrant of the globe. The expressions of our national goodwill achieved their most impressive results in western Europe and Japan, but the majority of the countries that were poor and illiterate in 1950 remain as they were before the advent of American idealism—still poor, still illiterate, still dependent for their subsistence on the sale of their forests and their children. If the wonders of modern communication make it possible for a Hollywood audience to watch the bombing of Afghanistan on CNN, they also invite the gaunt and hungry viewers in Cairo and Tashkent to look back through the media show window at the buffet tables on the beach at Malibu. Nobody needs to know the names of the celebrities to take the point. The pictures at the exhibition excite the passions of a transcendent cause among people, most of them not yet twenty, with nowhere to go and nothing to lose.

The events furnishing the headlines in recent months—the civil war in Israel as well as the subjugation of Iraq—speak to the rising surge of violence in the world, and we might wish to ask ourselves on what ethical ground do we defend our American freedom and prosperity? Nobody disputes the fact of our military and economic predominance, but with what moral and intellectual force do we confront the hostility of a world populated by increasing numbers of people who bear us no goodwill and maybe can find their way to weapons as terrible as our own?

The questions beg an answer, but among the coiners of our well-informed opinion they seldom even get asked. The television anchorpersons comfort us with flags and fairy tales; the White House and the Pentagon come forward with policy initiatives directed toward the way things were in 1945. Our politicians flee from ambiguity almost as hurriedly as they shun dissent, but should it occur to them to formulate an enlightened foreign policy, they might begin with the observation that America owes its wealth and power to the resources of the human intellect, not to the favor of God's will. The Republic that Benjamin Franklin knew would be hard to keep was conceived as the freedom from priests as well as kings, the strength of the idea founded on the capacity of its citizens to think and speak without cant and the success of the joint venture dependent upon the extent to which we try to tell each other the truth. The task was never an easy one, but it becomes more urgent in a New World Order dressed up in the robes of a spiritual revelation that regards the asking of too many questions as both unpatriotic and impious. Once bathed in Holy Water, and so cleansed of the sin of worldly politics, the government can send its crusader knights anywhere it chooses (to Panama or North Korea or Afghanistan) without referring the decision to a vote of the Congress or the will of the American people.

By confusing the glory of money with the spirit of liberty, our wastrel governments in Washington over the previous fifty years have been notably unsuccessful at promoting, either at home or abroad, the public virtues of citizenship, magnanimity, and self-restraint. We have distributed instead a more profitable line of private goods—hot tubs and F-16s as well as episodes of *Baywatch* and McDonald's cheeseburgers; the blessings that we cannot attribute directly to God, we assign to the Holy Ghost embodied in the miracle of the world's capital markets.[8] Unfortunately, and contrary to the upbeat messages from the sponsors, neither God nor His market

---

[8]Although intended as a hymn to America the Great and Good, the halftime show at February 2002's Super Bowl XXXVI was less impressive as an expression of a political idea than as a tribute to the divinity of the market forces that could change the death of 3,000 Americans on September 11 into a sales pitch for Coca-Cola. Billed as "A Celebration of America" and selling 131.7 million customers the good news that grief is a consumer product, the six-hour program (game and pregame entertainment) produced every trick of the media trade: opening on a wide shot of New Orleans from a NASA satellite camera in outer space, theme music borrowed from the soundtrack of *Star Wars,* film footage of America the beautiful (Mt. Rushmore, the White House, amber waves of grain), four ex-presidents reading from the speeches and letters of Abraham Lincoln, Paul McCartney playing the guitar and Mariah Carey singing "The Star-Spangled Banner," a reenactment of the raising of the flag on Iwo Jima, Don Shula and Michael Strahan on the roster of NFL players and coaches reading from the Declaration of Independence, festive greetings from a Marine unit in far-off Afghanistan ("the most heavily armed Super Bowl party in the world"), a Budweiser beer commercial in which the brewer's trademark Clydesdale horses bring their wagon to New York and kneel in homage to the diminished skyline; the halftime show was performed by Bono and his band against the backdrop of a diaphanous scrim bearing the names of people who had perished in the destruction of the World Trade Center—the names of firemen, airline passengers, policemen, office workers, all rising, like the credits on a movie screen, into the strobe-lit heavens of the Superdome.

can defend a city, write a new equation, commit an act of the moral or political imagination.

In an increasingly dangerous world the United States cannot escape the necessity of dealing with people who might not warrant membership in a Dallas golf club, but we make a bad mistake if we count upon the accommodating dictator to save us the trouble of risking our own lives, and when considering the chance of a policy or an alliance, we might learn to ask more searching questions of our newfound friend in the handsome military uniform—not "Are you with us or against us?" but "In what circumstances do we find those of your people not living in the palace? Do they walk upright on two feet in the manner of human beings or do they crouch on their hindquarters like humiliated dogs?" The simplicity of the distinction might prompt the makers of American foreign policy to weigh the worth of a nation's laws more heavily in the balance than an Arab sheikh's capacity to give an emerald to the wife of an oil company president. The more people who become fully human in the world, the fewer the hostages to fortune, and the less seductive the voices prophesying war.

July 2003

Caesar's Wives

Money does not rule democracy. Money is democracy.
—THOMAS BEER

*B*oth major political parties traveled to their nominating conventions last August with slush funds twice the size of the ones they had amassed for the election of 1996 ($137 million in the custody of the Republicans, $119 million at the discretion of the Democrats), and to citizens unacquainted with our native genius for the art of money laundering the timing might have seemed unfortunate. Never in the history of the republic was so much loose cash apt to be spilled on the carpets of liberty, but never in living memory had the conventions been preceded by so much solemn talk about the dire need for campaign finance reform.

Ever since President Clinton had been discovered renting rooms in the White House to guests palsied with the disease of special

interest, the country's editorial pages had been loud with moralizing condemnations—of Vice President Al Gore for shaking
down Buddhist nuns, of Newt Gingrich for selling the remnant
of his scruples to Rupert Murdoch, of numerous congressmen,
both Republican and Democrat, for feeding too noisily from the
soupspoons of the oil, banking, tobacco, and telecommunications
lobbies. For nearly three years no week had passed without a word
of rebuke from the pulpits of the Sunday-morning television
shows, and in the autumn of last year Senators Bill Bradley and
John McCain answered the trumpet of the opinion polls by allying
their presidential ambitions with the promise to disinfect the Oval
Office and scrub clean the marble halls of Congress. They carried
their message into the spring primary campaigns, and as recently
as last February, in Michigan and New Hampshire, McCain was
still astonishing rural crowds with his traveling salesman's display
of dust mops, air fresheners, and rubber gloves.

But now it was the summer of prosperity in Philadelphia and
Los Angeles, and the special interests weren't making things easy
for the laundry services of reform. The money was everywhere in
plain sight—flowing over the hotel bars, dressed prettily in silk
on the sofa of an executive suite, handed around on toast points
in the hospitality tents—and the commercial sponsors didn't
bother to conceal its origin or intent. In Philadelphia and again
in Los Angeles the same caucus of prominent corporations (General Motors, AT&T, Motorola, Hewlett-Packard, Microsoft, etc.,
etc.) arranged golf outings, paid for the music and the balloons.
The event lists in the two cities were somewhat different—the
Republicans comforted with Tiffany crystal and Mozart string

quartets, the Democrats with the singing of Barbra Streisand or the presence of John Travolta—but both parties made similarly fine distinctions between donors of large and small degree. The Democrats reserved the better invitations for members of the "Chairman's Circle," patrons who had furnished at least $500,000 since January 1999; the Republicans awarded the rank of "Regent" to contributors of $250,000, which in Philadelphia prompted a murmur of distress from the "Pioneers," who had limited their enthusiasm to amounts somewhat nearer $100,000. It was noticed that at the cocktail parties in the Four Seasons Hotel the Regents weren't herded into corners and that in the courtesy vans en route to White Marsh Valley Country Club they had more room to stretch their legs. When the victims of discrimination brought their sorrows to Mel Sembler, Florida shopping-center magnate and finance chairman of the Republican National Committee, he answered with a clarity of phrase that was missing from the speaker's podium in both convention halls.

"You pay a little more," Mel said, "you get a little more."

Although admirable both for its brevity and its axiomatic truth, so blunt a definition of American politics is not one that flatters the country's preferred image of itself. As descendants of the seventeenth-century Puritans who landed in Massachusetts Bay with the idea that they had regained the states of grace lost to Satan by corrupt and inattentive Europeans, we choose to believe that America is as innocent as Eden. Foreigners commit crimes against humanity; Americans make well-intentioned mistakes.

Foreigners incite wars, encourage terrorists, manufacture cocaine; Americans cleanse the world of its spiritual impurities. True, our corporations occasionally permit themselves the luxuries of thievery and fraud, but such crimes, being American and therefore subject to our special arrangement with Providence, can be understood as temporary breakdowns in the otherwise flawless machinery of the American soul. The fault is never one of motive, and our hearts are always pure.

The doctrines of American exceptionalism condemn us to the rituals of ceaseless purification that smooth the edges of our speech, dictate the terms of our foreign policy, describe most of what passes for our literature and public education. The nation spends as recklessly on soap as it does on weapons, the object of both expenditures being the protection of the American body politic against the contamination of alien substances. Self-respecting banks in every American city send millions of dollars each week to the purifying baths in Switzerland and the Bahamas, and every village drugstore stocks hundreds of lotions, perfumes, and spray colognes imbued with the scent of immortality. Our high school textbooks come cleansed of strong expression, the short nouns and active verbs softened with the euphemisms of political correctness; our food comes wrapped in plastic, cured of its imperfections and suffused with artificial colorings that disguise its association with animals.

Transferred into the political arena, the national sanitary codes oblige all candidates for public office to feign the clean-limbed idealism of college sophomores, wholesome and good-natured fellows who know little or nothing of ambition, lust, selfishness, and cowardly betrayal. The more daring members of the troupe might go so far as to admit having read about such awful things in the newspapers, but the incidents in question invariably have to do with somebody belonging to the other political party. We require our politicians to wear the masks of innocence, starch the shirt fronts of the American conscience, and remove the stains from capitalism's bloody sheets.

The heavy bundles of damp cashier's checks in Brentwood and Rittenhouse Square burdened the protectors of America's virtue with a task of no small proportion, but fortunately for the health of the republic they addressed it with the resolve of patriots, and by the end of the first night of the Republican Convention it was clear that nobody was going to have any trouble disposing of the empty party bags from Spago and Estée Lauder. The cleansing agents were convenient and risk-free, untainted by dangerous chemicals, and requiring neither hot nor cold water. Make sanctimony the detergent and shift the spin cycle from the impersonal to the personal. Substitute the moral lesson for the legislative act, and one could talk about character, integrity, honor, dignity; also about Mom, Dad, Cousin Juanita, and the kids. Lift the discourse into the spheres of pure abstraction, and the more profuse the piety, the less likely that any of the words might be mistaken for a statement of the facts. Let everybody concentrate on the storing up of treasure in Heaven, and maybe nobody would notice the squirreling away of the boodle here on Earth.

*   *   *

The program in both Philadelphia and Los Angeles could as easily have served the purposes of a nursery school Christmas pageant or a Girl Scout jamboree. Both conventions enforced strict rules of cleanliness, the Democrats forbidding a fund-raising event at the Playboy Mansion, the Republicans staging depositions in favor of domestic bliss, and during the month of August the wisdom vouchsafed to the voting republic under the heading of politics consisted mostly of home videos showing each of the four candidates to be a loving husband, dutiful father, faithful friend. None of them the kind of man who would cheat an orphan or kick a dog, and all of them, praised be the Lord, sexually inert.

What was impressive was the way in which everybody except Governor George Bush managed to keep a straight face. Most of the speakers standing up to the TelePrompTers had been bought and sold so many times that they might as well have been wearing canvas jumpsuits, similar to those worn by professional race-car drivers, stamped with every logo in the encyclopedia of American commercial enterprise. Their success as politicians followed from their trotting along behind the leashes of other people's money, and if they knew nothing else, they knew how to stomach humiliation and swallow insult with a frozen smile. And yet here they were in the band music and the television light, testimonials to the rewards of corporate servitude, talking about honor, trust, courage, and, best and most wonderful of all, dignity.

To each of the conventions the news media dispatched 15,000 journalists to help with the laundry, their number indicative of the extent of the labor at hand, and very few of them could afford to recall H. L. Mencken's remark about politicians being trained to know "the taste of the boot polish." The well-known delegates from the national press corps work for the same corporations (Viacom, Time Warner, Disney, etc.) that were supplying the smoked salmon and the limousines, and the better-informed members of the entourage knew that of the several billion dollars allocated to the current election season, 60 percent of the appropriation was being spent for print and television advertising. Nor was it convenient to the media's *amour-propre* to suggest that America was anything other than the land of the free and the home of the brave. If the nation's politics were to be seen as nothing more complicated than the market in pork bellies, what would become of their self-esteem? Who would listen to their Sunday sermons, and what would happen to the lecture fees?

Disinclined to quarrel with the official distributions of sentiment and excluded from the private receptions in which money might be changing hands (unless, of course, they agreed to say nothing about who was present or what was said), the principal media operatives confined their remarks to points of strategy and traits of character. Where was the trend in Oregon, and what were the focus groups saying in Kansas? The television correspondents sat around the skyboxes gossiping about Senator Joseph Leiberman's Jewishness ("What do you think, Peggy, a plus or a minus?"), about Tipper's shoes and Laura's dress, about the godlike manifestation of General Norman Schwarzkopf on the deck of the USS *New Jersey* ("A grand old lady, Tom, the most decorated ship in the Navy"). The important columnists adopted the manner of visiting clergymen, and instead of writing about the prices being paid for the privilege of composing next year's federal guidelines

for the insurance and communications industries, they wrestled
with the questions of personal conduct and deportment. Does the
man drink? Will he keep his hands off the secretaries? When was
the last time he spoke to Jesus?

As the candidates approached the evening of their triumphant
nominations the newspaper prose tended to become increasingly
sunny. The effect was especially noticeable in the *New York Times*.
Long ago in February, when it looked as if Governor Bush might
lose yet another primary election to Senator John McCain, the
paper portrayed him as a dull-witted lout, hesitant and uncertain,
knowing little of politics, taking his cues from his father's former
privy councillors. By early April he had acquired the stature of a
surprisingly effective speaker, and by late May his accomplishments as governor of Texas were seen to be both statesmanlike
and well considered. During the week prior to his coming to
Philadelphia the *Times* published a daily report of his progress
eastward from the Mississippi River, strewing his path with adjectives of gradually higher quality, and then, on the morning
after his entrance into the city famous for the Liberty Bell, the
paper welcomed him on its front page as a man of "dazzling
charm, tremendous social skills, a bold self-confidence, growing
political savvy, great popularity . . ."

The governor on August 3 apparently stood a better than even
chance of becoming the next president of the United States, and
how else do the media earn their keep (also their free gift of the
nation's broadcast frequencies) if not by flattering the wealth and
wisdom in office? Money is the American Caesar, the sovereign
power whose whim is law, and although I know a good many

people who complain of the arrangement, I don't see that it allows for much argument.

During the week between the conventions I happened to read Thomas Beer's biography of Mark Hanna, the Ohio coal merchant who successfully purchased, in 1896 and again in 1900, the presidential election for Major William McKinley. Both Hanna and his biographer were as candid as Mel Sembler about the terms of the American political contract, and the book deserves a place on the reading lists at Harvard. At the turn of the twentieth century Hanna bought votes as openly as his fellow plutocrats bought railroad rolling stock, and Beer, writing in 1928, understood that the American Revolution had put an end to the old feudal and mercantile systems of morality. Dead judges of the King's Bench could not impose a Christian conscience on large capital "in the hands of men without traditions and bound to no caste," could not control "this floating, detached mass of power which illusively seemed free of the earth." Democracy created American capitalists, as American capital created democracy, and if we live in a society in which the rich govern the poor, it is because we possess no other authority capable of doing so—no aristocracy, no church, no educated class loyal to a code of civic duty.

But we don't like to be reminded of the fact. Somewhere in the attic of our Puritan memory we retain the portrait of money as a vile slumlord, ungodly and depraved, and the more wealth that the society accumulates the more obsessive our ritual washing of the currency. We didn't use to be so fussy about the behavior and moral rectitude of Caesar's wives. Hanna's politicians were allowed to smoke cigars and spit on the floors.

The ancient Romans became more meticulous about the shows of public virtue as their empire embraced more nakedly the joys of private vice, and if the American stock markets continue to perform the miracle of the loaves and the fishes, I see no reason why our presidential candidates shouldn't meet the specifications set for other consumer products by the Food and Drug Administration. At Philadelphia and Los Angeles the four nominees did their best to portray themselves as soccer moms or pet rabbits, but still the pictures were less than perfect. The money staying in the better hotels complained about a general lack of imperial refinement—the wrong kind of chocolate on the pillows, the music a little loud, too many golfers on the bus—and before long it undoubtedly will demand of its consorts standards of deportment more decorously chaste, levels of emotion more delicately feminine. Let the Dow Jones average rise another 4,000 points, and four or eight years from now we can look forward to seeing the candidates in the milk-white robes of vestal virgins, and instead of balloons falling from the rafters of the convention halls, rose petals and the scent of lilies.

October 2000

Cleopatra's Nose

The Inevitable is what will seem to happen to you purely by
  chance;
The Real is what will strike you as really absurd;
Unless you are certain you are dreaming, it is certainly a
  dream of your own;
Unless you exclaim—"There must be some mistake"—you
  must be mistaken.
                    —W. H. AUDEN

O n the first day of what was billed as the Millennium Sum-
    mit last September in New York, Kofi Annan, Secretary-
    General of the United Nations, welcomed the assembled
dignities from 147 countries (prime ministers, heads of state,
crowned kings) with a banquet and the proposing of a toast to
"You [who] have the authority to speak for, and the ability to
transform, the lives of six billion people."

The flattery was extravagant—at most times and places in the
history of the world politicians have followed the trends and
obeyed the polls, distinguished by their expedient silences and
mortal fear of transformations—but it was cheerfully received

(strong applause, complacent nods), and for three days and three nights the dignities gave speeches, ratified treaties, glanced at documents, signed declarations of blameless principle in favor of human freedom and the biosphere.

The coming and going of limousines imparted an air of triumph to the proceedings, and because I spent a good deal of time marooned in traffic during the first week of September, learning to rate the importance of the personage in the motorcade by the number of vans bearing pastry chefs or secret service agents, I was often at leisure to read dispatches from U.N. headquarters on the East River and to reflect on the postmodern theories of global empire.

Our twenty-first-century faith in scientific miracle gives rise to the hope of "transnational institutions" capable of managing the world's affairs with the sangfroid of the late and increasingly lamented emperor Caesar Augustus. His latter-day heirs and assigns, most of them corporation executives, find themselves confronted with rebellion in provincial capital markets—also with rogue states and renegade ideologies, with war in Africa, civil unrest in Judaea, tyrants in Parthia and Leptis Minor, too much cocaine crossing the frontier near Chalcedon—and the would-be makers of a computer-enhanced Pax Romana dream of a Supreme Magistrate, "invested," in Edward Gibbon's phrase, "with the sublime perfections of an Eternal Parent, and an Omnipotent Monarch."

On the podium of the General Assembly the dignities talked mostly about political economy, about "bridging the gulf" (also "narrowing the distance," and "breaking down the walls") between the nations of the rich and the nations of the poor, but no matter

how different the geographical perspective or the ideological in-
flection—Fidel Castro denouncing the "abusive and unfair order"
imposed by the "hegemonic superpower" on its Third World serfs
and vassals; President Clinton suggesting that because "everyone
counts, everyone has a role to play"—all present endorsed the
belief in a predictable future subject to corporate purchase, technological advance, and government decree. With enough money
and a modicum of goodwill, surely the obstacles could be over-
come, a more equitable division of the world's wealth arranged by
well-meaning technical advisers (prize-winning physicists, eminent scholars, handsome anchorpersons, etc.), the wilderness of
contingent and random event domesticated with decisions by
committee.

It wasn't only the front-page news that mocked the presumptions
of omnipotence—civil war in Colombia and Sierra Leone, famine
in Ethiopia, a mob armed with machetes murdering three U.N.
officials in West Timor (on the same day that Kofi Annan was
raising his glass of congratulatory champagne), civil war in
Chechnya and Sri Lanka, floods in India and six men arrested for
cannibalism in Tanzania. Elusive messages elsewhere in the paper
offered possibly more telling instances of a world indifferent to
the rules of parliamentary procedure—open water at the North
Pole, 11 million lobsters dead in Long Island Sound; in California
a colony of Argentine ants 600 miles long; *Caulerpa taxifolia,* a
tropical algae bright green in color and apparently escaped from
the aquarium in Monaco, inexorably suffocating the plants on the

floor of the Mediterranean Sea; severe drought in Texas, an unusual number of forest fires in Montana, in Colorado an inexplicable proliferation of bears.

A second story about the thinning of the polar ice (its weight and mass reduced by 58 percent over the last fifty years) appeared on page 3 in the *New York Times* on the same day that Maumoon Gayoom, president of the Maldives, spoke to the U.N. General Assembly about the possible consequences of rising sea levels for the low-lying islands in the Indian Ocean. "Not only a sobering thought," he said, "but an alarming one," and the wistful tenor of his remark reminded me of what is known as "the butterfly effect," the belief among proponents of string and chaos theory that everything in the world is somehow mysteriously intercon- nected and so finely balanced that a slight, seemingly insignificant, flutter of a butterfly's wing on a Swiss Alp can provoke a typhoon in the South China Sea; the French philosopher Blaise Pascal ex- pressed the idea as a succinct *pensée*—"Cleopatra's nose, had it been shorter, the whole aspect of the world would have been changed"; contemporary historians account for the effect under the heading of "What If?" and I was familiar with some of the long chains of counterfactual sequence inferred from a different result at a famous crossroads of military victory and defeat. If a northeast wind does not blow across Brooklyn Heights on the evening of August 29, 1776, George Washington loses the Continental Army, and the American Revolution fails; the Mongols sack Vienna and overrun Europe if in the winter of 1242 the army of the Golden Horde isn't suddenly obliged to return to Karakorum for the funeral of the Great Khan, Ogodai.

Although by no means given to republican practice or democratic sentiment, the Emperor Augustus understood the uses of
poets, the fictions of government, the glory of apple trees, and at
the end of the first century B.C. he undertook to civilize the wilderness of Germany-Across-the-Rhine with the force of arms and
a show of aqueducts. He had it in mind to extend the empire as
far north as the Elbe River, possibly as far east as the Vistula and
the Baltic Sea, to reduce the Teutonic hordes, as Julius Caesar
had reduced the Gauls west and south of the Rhine to a province
of submissive colonies "well supplied with luxuries and accustomed to defeat." The policy was optimistic but not implausible,
and if the emperor's legions had not lost the Battle of the Teu-
toburg Forest in the autumn of A.D. 9 (leaving the barbarians un-
molested by amphitheaters and well supplied with spears and
drinking songs), the course of European history over the next
2,000 years might have taken a very different set of turns—the
Roman Empire preserved from ruin, Christ dying intestate on an
unremembered cross, the non-appearance of the English language, neither the need nor the occasion for a Protestant refor-
mation, Frederick the Great a circus dwarf, Kaiser Wilhelm
seized by an infatuation with stamps and water beetles instead of
a passion for cavalry boots, Adolf Hitler, an obscure painter of
harmless watercolors.

A similarly speculative spirit informs Jane Jacobs's book *The Nature of Economies*, which correlates the butterfly effect to the wealth
and poverty of nations, and which, not by accident, I happened

to be reading during the week when the dignitaries were in town. Jacobs addresses a category of questions allied with those that were being discussed at the General Assembly, and she directs her argument to the unfortunately high percentage of otherwise intelligent people (many of them prime ministers, crowned kings and heads of state) who make the mistake of classifying economics as a department of mathematics rather than as a life science. The shuffling of budgets across or under the desks of the World Bank results in the " 'Thing Theory' of development" dear to the hearts of government officials who see the impoverished nations of the earth as unimproved properties on a Monopoly board. They add expensive infrastructure (hydroelectric dams, oil refineries, copper mines) to satisfy the requirements of the people advancing the capital but fail to answer to the needs of the people supplying the labor.

On the last day of the summit meetings, Robert Mugabe, the dictator-president of Zimbabwe, seconded the motion in stronger language, the resentments implicit in his rhetoric suggesting that the road to what Tony Blair of Britain blithely described as "a better future in Africa" was not likely to be paved with paper protocols:

If the new Millennium, like the last, remains an age of hegemonic empires and conquerors doing the same old things in new technological ways, remains the age of the master race, the master economy and the master state, then I am afraid we in developing countries will have to stand up as a matter of principle and say, "Not again."

Principles unsupported by the energies of a sustainable economy stand only at the whim of somebody else's politics or money, and Jacobs would have us learn to imitate the production methods found in nature. Like all other living organisms—football teams, estuaries, insurance companies, glial and phagocytic cells—economies exist in the state of constant self-correction, adjusting to circumstances, inventing the future with instruments for which nobody ever thought to place an order with General Electric or The Walt Disney Company. Jacobs draws the analogy between a prolific rain forest and a prosperous city—two applications of the same principle, two compositions for "self-organized ensemble," two variations, both impromptu, on the themes of unintended consequences. Understand the economy of the forest, and you understand the ecology of the city, or, vice versa and equally instructive, recognize the city as natural habitat, and you discover the forest as sophisticated artifact. Men assemble automobiles, and beavers build dams; the constructions owe their existence to, and become extensions of, a living organism. Bees inhabit a world of their own manufacture; so do subscribers to the Internet. The projects of human technology exist wholly within nature, evolving, like anthills, from a set of circumstances that they can neither invent nor transcend.

Jacobs marvels at the abundant proofs of ingenuity displayed by honey birds as well as metallurgists, and she wonders whether it might not be possible to build economic mechanisms as benignly biodegradable as the walls of Troy or the bones of Vlad the Impaler. An abalone manufactures first-rate ceramics at life-friendly temperatures despite its ignorance of chemistry and lack of a diploma from MIT. Why then do the friends of the free market—clever with their hands, rich in laboratories, more widely traveled than most abalones—not do likewise?

The questions didn't show up in the briefing books at the Millennium Summit. Not only do they cast doubt on the habits of thought implicit in imperial economic planning (i.e., that the future is stable, uniform, and for sale) but they also insult the majesty of science and disagree with the presumption that we can anticipate events, eliminate uncertainty, reconfigure the accidents of climate and geography. About the arts of political economy we have more to learn from bakers, architects, and horticulturists than from bankers and finance ministers, but we choose to believe that we inhabit a virtual reality somewhere at a safe distance from the vagaries of nature, and by making an excessive number of self-important distinctions between what is natural and what is artificial, we invest our technologies with the powers that the old Romans assigned to gods—either the sublime perfection of an Eternal Parent or the deadly purpose of alien automatons destroying the happiness of daffodils and unborn trout.

Both forms of worship diminish the range of our initiative and creativity. Jacobs makes the point with a story about the Alabama hairdresser and the 11 million gallons of oil spilled by the *Exxon Valdez* in Alaska's Prince William Sound. The company spent $2 billion over a period of four years to recover only 12 percent of the drifting oil; the hairdresser saw a photograph of a dying otter, thought about its saturated fur, and began experimenting with bundles of hair clippings that he swept from the floor of his salon, soaked with motor oil and floated in his son's wading pool. Eventually he found a method that in seven days would have cleaned up the whole of the *Valdez* spill with the sweepings of 200,000 American barbershops done up in mesh pillows.

Add to the degrees of uncertainty the unfathomable ecosystems of the human brain—multiplying at the rate of organelles and the *Anopheles* mosquito, capable of bringing forth the cantatas of Johann Sebastian Bach or the chimneys at Dachau, and the numbers in the equations speak to the expansion of what the essayist Loren Eiseley once called "The Unexpected Universe," flickering unseen behind every whirl of our machines and every pronouncement of political or economic policy. Contingency has escaped into human hands, the emergent energies in the realm of mind as prolific and unstable as those in the kingdom of matter, but the gigantic organism that we now call the global economy stumbles into the future on a road marked only with the signposts of corporate purchase and technological advance. Flattered by a news and entertainment media that comforts us with proofs of our omnipotence (strong applause, complacent nods), we close the curtains against the invisible and procreant void and play with the maquettes of Rome reborn. We invest $50 billion in a missile defense system made entirely of metaphors, erect statues of the American Express card, bless our children in the baptismal font of the Internet.

We might as well be sacrificing goats on the altars of Poseidon, but so devout is our faith in "killer aps" that we omit the ritual gestures of humility. Roman generals returning from victories in

Illyricum or Cisalpine Gaul approached the Forum in the company of a centurion standing behind them in the chariot to remind them of their mortality; Elizabethan merchants drawing up contracts for the delivery of French cannon or Spanish wine hedged their signatures with the phrase "by the mutability of Fortune and Favor." The staff officers at the U.N. pour champagne.

November 2000

The Dimpled Chad

When I die—if I die—I want to be buried in Louisiana so I can
stay active in politics.
—EARL K. LONG

*U*ntil the presidential election ran afoul of events in Florida in the early morning of November 8, the interested
parties had managed to keep the politics out of the politics—behind the rope lines, off the podium, out of the camera
shots and the conversation. For nearly twelve months the Republican and Democratic campaigns had assumed that in place of
politics—a word they associated with "partisan ugliness" and
"angry name-calling"—they could substitute handsomely framed
photo opportunities and winsomely edited television commercials.
Why not? Who would care?

The country apparently was at ease with itself, enjoying its
prosperity and content with its toys; no wars loomed on a distant
horizon, and the presumed apathy of a supposedly ignorant elec-

torate suggested a general preference for a government so securely checked and balanced that it could do nothing that might upset the golden applecart of the Dow Jones Industrial Average.

What was wanted was a POTUS conveniently impotent, and the requirement favored the qualities of Governor George W. Bush and Vice President Al Gore—two ornamental sons of the American plutocracy bearing well-known national brand names and with as little difference between them as Pepsi and Coke, both capable of cameo appearances on *Oprah* and well enough schooled in the art of foraging for money to know where to stand and when to crawl.

If neither candidate commanded a broad or popular following among the American people, what difference did it make? The trend of the times over the last twenty years has reduced the figure of the president of the United States from a leading to a supporting role, and either the Governor or the Vice President would pass muster as the corporate spokesman for America the Beautiful. Maybe they weren't as good at making the pitch as either Ronald Reagan or Bill Clinton, but at least they could memorize a script, hit their marks, know their place, and because each of them so often found it necessary to say that he was his own man, even the dullest voter would be encouraged to understand that he wasn't. Surely the country was safe enough and rich enough to afford the luxury of two gentlemen from Verona or the Ivy League so amiably lacking in conviction that their words could be relied upon to mean as little as possible.

*   *   *

Any other year and the modest sets of accomplishment might have proved sufficient. Neither candidate fell off a bandstand or a parade float; the Vice President discovered the secret of studio makeup, the Governor learned how to pronounce the name Slobodan Milosevic, and over the course of the summer campaigns they obligingly displayed their talents as character actors in the various personae of visiting clergyman, bedside companion, late-night talk-show clown. Drawn by the gravitational force of the opinion polls to the still center of amiable consensus (i.e., the great good American place where nothing changes and everybody gets rich), both candidates cheerfully avoided most of the topics apt to excite controversy, and with regard to the standard operating procedures of the oil, banking, and telecommunications monopolies they were as silent as the ball washers at a country-club golf tournament. Resolute in their opposition to breast cancer, forthright in their commitment to dignity and leadership, uncompromising in their support of better days, bluer skies, and secure retirement, they were always glad to pose for Kodak moments on an aircraft carrier or a kindergarten chair. Most importantly, they put to rest any lingering suspicions that they might be interested in politics as an experiment with anything dangerous or new.

Not a brilliant campaign, but adequate to its purpose, and one that under ordinary circumstances would have resolved itself into the customary victory celebration (many balloons, joyful applause) and the corollary concession speech (scattered tears, noble melancholy). By the time the polls opened on Election Day the prospect of a vote "too close to call" presented the news media with a better show than anybody had thought possible after the summer nominating conventions. The television anchorpersons inflated the sporting analogies as soon as the polls closed on the East Coast— Tom Brokaw promising his viewers a wild and thrilling roller-coaster ride through the theme park of American history; Dan Rather announcing a contest "hot enough to peel house paint."

During the first few hours of the nationwide count of the election returns, the mood in the broadcast booths remained upbeat and sunny. For two weeks the studio people had been promoting the drama of narrow margins on the assumption that they were hyping an otherwise mediocre story about two second-tier celebrities, and they didn't draw too careful a distinction between democracy as a system of government and democracy as a form of entertainment—"Here we all are in Democracyland, folks! Stay tuned! Don't go away! We'll be right back with Cokie and Jeff and Rutherford B. Hayes!" Accustomed to believing themselves the creators of the character of the American president (whether the role happens to be played by Michael Douglas on HBO, Richard Nixon on the History Channel, Bill Clinton on C-Span, or Harrison Ford on Cinemax), the news and entertainment media had seen the summer campaigns as an audition for a four-year gig in the Oval Office. The White House set by now has become as familiar as Jerry Seinfeld's apartment or the booth on *Monday Night Football,* and the political analysts know where to look for the Marine helicopter and the portrait of George Washington. When obliged to drum up interest in national affairs, they ask questions not much different from those of the film critics. How will next season's situation comedy differ from the undignified burlesque of the Bill Clinton show? Is it an action movie or sentimental melodrama along the lines of NBC's *The West Wing*? How many women in the cast, and is the national security adviser insane?

Which was more or less the tone of the complacent commentary on MSNBC and at CNN headquarters in Atlanta until something began to go wrong with the news from Florida. Nobody knew who was making what kind of mistakes—some difficulties, apparently, with missing ballots, faulty voting machines, confused pensioners—but by 3:00 A.M. it had begun to look as if the election wasn't going to follow the studio scripts, and after having twice awarded the prize of Florida's electoral votes and the presidency to the wrong candidate, the anchorpersons in the broadcast booths were showing a marked resemblance to aquarium fish. Their mouths were opening and closing; they were floating around in their state-of-the-art habitat, the red-and-blue maps as colorful as tiny coral reefs, but when they peered into the glass wall of the camera, it was as if they were wondering what had happened to the Caribbean Sea.

Astonishingly, and for the first time in twelve months, the election news was about something other than Al Gore's hairstyle or George Bush's English springer spaniel. Few of the people in the broadcast studios were old enough to remember ever having seen such a thing as democracy—the living organism as opposed to the old paintings and the marble statues—and judging by the startled expressions in their faces, they didn't like the look of it. It hadn't been circumcised, and probably it was criminal.

*   *   *

By noon on Wednesday the politics were back in the politics, pushing through the rope lines and crowding into the camera shots. The election still being in doubt, the interested parties were off message and out of costume, and for the next several days the impromptu course in civics was comprehensive; if I don't have the space to mention all the points in the syllabus, two of them seemed especially instructive:

THE CANDIDATES

Revealed as popped balloons and empty boasts. Without a script neither the Vice President nor the Governor knew what to say, and as the days passed, their wax images melted in the sun. The fine phrases (about "leadership," "restoring honor and dignity to the White House," "fighting for working families," "compassionate conservatism," etc., etc.) went missing in action. The two gentlemen from Verona elected to hide. Governor Bush retreated to his Texas ranch to pose for photographs in what he hoped was a presidential sort of way, among the props of a jury-rigged White House Map Room. During the campaign he had acknowledged his dependence on the advice of his father's senior bagmen (he knew their telephone numbers and promised to get in touch if something important came up), and when confronted with the possible loss of the election in Florida, he sent James A. Baker III, his father's former secretary of state, to fix the judge.

The Vice President retired into a cloud of piety. Not having Colin Powell for a prop, he appeared briefly for the cameras with a football that maybe once had been tossed around a Virginia lawn by Jack or Bobby Kennedy. Like the Governor, the Vice President sought to convey an air of Olympian calm, as indifferent as Zeus to the struggles of merely mortal men and so devoted to democracy's holy cause that he didn't wish to win the presidency "by a few votes cast in error." He went on to say that he was sure Governor Bush, that great and loyal American, would take the same view of the matter, and the gorgeous sweetness of his hypocrisy was a wonder to behold.

THE ELECTORATE

By no means as apathetic as it is customarily supposed by the Washington gentry and their attendant pundits, who conceive of democratic self-government as an heirloom or a trust fund, a theatrical trunk in which to find the costumes of an imaginary and risk-free past rather than as a blueprint and a source of energy with which to build a new and therefore dangerous future.

Once the politics were in plain sight, out from behind the screen of the soft-focus television commercials and the Hallmark greeting-card chatter of the Sunday talk-show crowd, a very large number of people expressed a keen and well-informed interest in the proceedings. They knew what they were looking at, knew also that "partisan ugliness" is the bone and marrow of democracy.

All at once and without cue cards, the liveliness of the political debate was a match for the barroom discussions of a World Series or a Super Bowl. High school students who a week earlier would have been hard-pressed to name three American presidents, living or dead, suddenly were talking, and talking knowledgeably, about the Electoral College, the Fourteenth Amendment, and the prior-arrest records of select Florida politicians. Every news organization, daily paper as well as the radio and cable-television networks, reported audiences four and six times as large as those that had attended the O. J. Simpson trial or the funeral of Princess Di. Although various important persons, most of them government officials, stepped up to a microphone to suggest that one of the candidates graciously resign (for the sake of a democracy so fragile that it might get broken if somebody tried to take it out of the museum), the guests on the Leno and Letterman shows (more representative of the broader spectrum of American opinion) were asking one another why the Bush and Gore campaigns had forgotten to register the graveyard vote.

All present on both sides of the argument filed amicus curiae briefs in favor of high-minded sentiment (for the good of the country, on behalf of the Constitution), but in the context of a real argument taking place in real time with a real consequence in the offing, it wasn't hard to notice that the most selfless principle was usually the one that served the most selfish motive. Thus the Republican congressman Connie Mack, affronted by the spectacle of Democrats actually trying to win the election—"They're politicizing the political process." Or Governor Bush's man Baker, pompous and indignant, complaining about "mischief" and "human error" as if politics ever had consisted of anything else.

Ordinary citizens took the points more quickly than the legal and academic authorities delivering sermons from the pulpit of an op-ed page, and the more interesting commentary tended to show up on a newspaper letters page rather than on the network news broadcasts. Here were the American people, for the most part good-natured and patient, working their way around the lies to the harder and better questions that had been ignored or suppressed by the managers of the brightly packaged presidential campaigns. Who gets to say when the voting stops? To whom do we assign political sovereignty—to the polls or the courts? If the latter jurisdiction, then to a federal or a state court? Maybe it isn't such a good idea to form a government so securely checked and balanced that it becomes both harmless and inert? Maybe the country is neither rich enough nor safe enough to afford the weakness of two playpen politicians who don't know how to either win or steal an election?

Judging by what I could see or infer from the all-but-continuous television transmissions from Florida, the local political people (state senators, trial judges, members of county canvassing boards) were more seriously committed to the idea of democracy than were the Washington grandees extending the courtesy of a dissembling press conference. Unexpectedly, and against the grain of my own sarcasm, I was as moved as I was impressed by the sight of the precinct workers holding paper ballots up to the light, looking to see whether the chad was dimpled or bulged, hanging by two threads or three. The tactical circumstance obligated the Republican strategists to scorn them for their "shenanigans" and to mock them for their innocence. Mere human beings, said Mr. Baker and Mr. Bush, imperfect and subjective, incapable of meeting the uniform standards of a machine. The assertion served its expedient purpose, but the condescension missed the point. Democracy isn't made by a machine; it is made with the wit and courage of citizens willing to undertake, for low pay and no credit, a tedious and time-consuming search for a straight answer in a little square of perforated light.

As of this present writing the election remains in doubt, and it's not inconceivable that the next president of the United States will be named by the Supreme Court or the House of Representatives. But if nobody can guess what happens next, we know from the lesson chalked up on the tote boards in Florida that we live in an energetic democracy that at least gives us a sporting chance at an inventive future—whether we rig it with persuasive speeches, artful lawsuits, or a dimpled chad.

January 2001

Civics Lesson

[A free people has] an indisputable, unalienable, indefeasible,
divine right to that most dreaded and envied kind of knowledge,
I mean of the characters and conduct of their rulers.
—JOHN ADAMS

*D*uring the month when the presidential election was still
a work in progress, the television footage from Washington and Tallahassee provided hourly updates of
Adams's "most dreaded and envied kind of knowledge," and for
nearly forty days and forty nights we had a chance to see what we
mean by the phrases "the rule of law" and "democratic self-government." Opinions differed as to whether the course of instruction was worth the harm done to our notion of free and fair
elections, and for many years to come I expect to be reading books
explaining how and why it came to pass that the Supreme Court
appointed George W. Bush to the office of president.

Authors in liberal jurisdictions undoubtedly will cite passages
from the Florida civics lesson as the premise for treatises on the

fall of the American empire or the ruin of the American republic. Apostles of the conservative revelation conceivably will cite the same testimony as preface to five-volume histories of America's moral reawakening. My own view is more haphazard and less apocalyptic—a sequence of preliminary observations rather than the components of a theory or a conclusion.

When the Florida ballot on November 8 failed to find in favor of either candidate, the news media swarmed to the occasion with so many cameras and talking heads that the shape of the story was as quickly lost as that of a dead buffalo under a veil of shrieking crows. At every hour of the day and night the all but ceaseless commentary tended to obscure rather than illuminate the text, and I knew that I was likely to forget what I was being told unless I kept a fairly extensive set of notes. I didn't follow all the lines of all the legal maneuvers. Every motion filed by both parties to the dispute proceeded from the assumption that if all the votes cast in Florida somehow could be accurately counted, Vice President Al Gore probably would win the election, and I was content to stipulate what was attested to by the lack of argument on the point. Why else did the Republicans seek to stop, impede, indefinitely postpone, any revisiting of the ballots? They never tired of accusing the Democrats of trying to steal the election ("Chad Molesters!" "Commanders in Thief!"), but it was their own behavior that was more obviously suspect, hurrying to get the votes across the border and out of state before somebody searched their luggage.

Mostly I was interested in traits of character, and on reviewing my own brief I notice that I weighted the emphasis toward the furious confusion in the minds of the Republicans-who-would-be-king. I could understand their wanting to carry Mr. Bush in triumph to the White House (as if he were the family silver or a baseball signed by Babe Ruth), and I could appreciate their sense of urgency and haste. But why were they always enraged? They controlled almost all of the political machinery in Florida (the legislature, the governor's office, the state government, the Cuban diaspora), and yet they imagined themselves unfairly persecuted by a jealous god and wicked trolls. What was it to which they believed themselves entitled, and how did they arrive at the certain knowledge of their own virtue?

I never came up with clear answers to the questions, but now that the country has been placed in the care of Mr. Bush's tutors, I expect that I'll be returning to them at frequent intervals over the next four years, and if I'm at a loss to understand a point of national policy—why we're at war with China, or what happened to the forests in Oregon—I can recall the sight of James A. Baker III on the evening of November 21, angrily informing a press conference in Tallahassee that the Florida Supreme Court had committed what he construed to be the crime of lese majesty. The court had handed down a decision of which Mr. Baker disapproved—to permit the recounting, by hand, of undervoted ballots in three Florida counties—and therefore, in Mr. Baker's view, the decision was null and void. A ruling by "judicial fiat," he said; insolent and not to be endured. The expression in his face—pinched, vengeful, and mean—I could assign to a choleric temperament or a display of tactical emotion on the part of a clever bully. What surprised me was the strength of his conviction. The

man apparently believed what he was saying, a rich lawyer in-
veighing against the rule of law, inciting the Florida legislature
to overturn (by a fiat more to Mr. Baker's liking) the judgment
of the court. Watching him read his statement, I understood that
he conceived of the law as a nuisance, an idiot tangle of "legalistic
language," superfluous and tiresome, that mostly served as a re-
course for people too poor or too weak to buy what they wished
or do as they pleased.

What frightened Mr. Baker was the prospect of the country's
democratic institutions falling into the hands of the wrong people—i.e., anybody unpersuaded by the holy writ of orthodox Re-
publicanism—and so he perceived the uses of political power as
primarily defensive. The laws were forms of crowd control, meant
to inhibit, punish, and restrict. Like Dick Cheney (saying dismis-
sively to an impertinent newspaper reporter, "You've had your
question"), or Katherine Harris, the Florida secretary of state (refusing to accept the revised tally from Palm Beach County because
the paperwork was ninety minutes late), or the Supreme Court
justices (silencing the presumptuous continuation of the Florida
election by a 5–4 vote), the custodians of the Republican conscience interpreted the power of government not as creative agency
or constructive force but as the power to suppress and deny—the
power of the customs official, the traffic judge, the police sergeant.

The great truth proclaimed through clenched teeth by Mr. Baker
in Tallahassee guided the Republican operatives in Florida to a
strategy summed up in the phrase "Unless we win, it's illegal."

Quick to impugn the character and motives of their opponents, they seldom missed the chance for malicious slander. A court that ruled in favor of Governor Bush was a court deserving of compliance and respect; a court that ruled otherwise was a treasonous court, renegade and corrupt. As with the courts, so also with judges, town clerks, members of county canvassing boards. Citizens allied with Governor Bush or the prima facie righteousness of the Republican cause deserved the name of "patriot." Democrats were "partisan hacks," by definition crooked and self-serving, slum-dwelling perps accustomed to stealing elections and cars.

I don't think I'm misreading the record. The feverish rhetoric shows up in my notes both as paraphrase and direct quotation, incessantly repeated throughout the month of November by Republican politicians in Washington and Florida. If it wasn't Mr. Baker broadly hinting at likely instances of theft and fraud, then it was Congressman Tom DeLay or Senator Trent Lott threatening "unelected judges" with charges of conspiracy. Even Governor Bush, frowning darkly in far-off Texas, was prompted to say that he didn't think it was right (no sir, not right at all) for an election to be "usurped."

The voices of Republican alarm in the print and television media upgraded the rhetoric to the pitch of near hysteria. The *Wall Street Journal*'s lead editorial accused the Democrats of attempting a "coup d'état." Excited columnists elsewhere on the page likened Al Gore to Adolf Hitler and Al Capone; every Democratic legal argument was "preposterous" or "illegitimate," every filing of a motion on Mr. Gore's behalf "an unfolding miscarriage of justice." When Jesse Jackson addressed a crowd in Palm Beach County, the paper discerned the threat of an organized putsch by rabble-rousing thugs. When a mob of Republican Party functionaries (several of them hired by Congressman DeLay) staged a riot in Miami-Dade County, the paper saw a quorum of true and loyal Americans standing up for free speech and the rights of man.

National Review on December 4 published the confession of Jay Nordlinger, one of its New York editors, who had taken a temporary leave of absence to write speeches for the Bush campaign and who had suffered dreadful torment on election night in Austin. Nordlinger told the story of how he had gone to bed "full of fear" and grim foreboding, certain that he would awaken to the news of Mr. Gore's accession to the White House. He knew that something bad was bound to happen because Democrats were born cheats and instinctive liars and therefore "better at politics than we are . . . better at fraud," unscrupulous people "ten feet tall," just like the Russians during the Cold War.

Equally distraught writers marked up other pages in the magazine with the entire catechism of Republican fear and loathing. A columnist by the name of Mark Steyn found the goodness of the American heart in the inland states colored red on November's electoral map; the color blue indicated the "debauched dystopias" on the nation's coastlines "that the rest of us can visit for wild weekends every now and again before returning to our homes in solid, enduring, conservative . . . America." Puzzled and disturbed by the unexpectedly large number of voters who had preferred the Democratic candidate, Steyn asked himself the question, "Who *are* these people?" and fortunately discovered, much to his relief, that most of them were misfits, criminals, and foreigners—"aliens Al

Gore strong-armed the INS into hustling through the naturalization process without background checks," also the friends of Al Sharpton and Alec Baldwin, senile pensioners rounded up from nursing homes, "gay scoutmasters," and "partial-birth-abortion fetishists," "the Palm Beach chapter of Jews for Buchanan."

The poisonous language dribbling out of the mouths of people who as recently as last summer had been talking about restoring "civility" to the American political discussion somehow seemed to me less surprising than the paranoid romance from which the plaintiffs apparently derived the casus belli for their imbecile remonstrance. They tell themselves a fairy tale, engaged in deadly combat with they know not what:

> The Vice President of the United States receives a plurality of the popular vote, and the Republican fantasts portray him as a jack-booted tyrant seizing a Latin American army or a Bulgarian radio station.

> The Clinton Administration for eight years bestows on the country's corporate clients the blessings of the China Trade Bill, repeal of the Glass-Steagall Act, low-cost labor, high stock-market prices, lenient interpretation of the anti-trust laws, reduced welfare payments to the poor, and in the minds of Rupert Murdoch's editorial writers the Clinton Administration is a sinister cabal sacking the temple of Mammon.

The nation enjoys the comforts of a timid and predominantly conservative news media (the four television networks and most of the cable channels, Time Warner, *USA Today*, nine of ten radio talk stations, etc., etc.), and on the foreheads of Kewpie-doll anchorpersons earning upwards of $2 million a year the fierce polemicists at The Heritage Foundation stamp the labels "Left-wing!" "Liberal!" "Anarchist!"

Maybe I was laboring under an unexamined bias, but I didn't find the same sort of stupidity on the Democratic side of the dispute. Not that the Democrats didn't reserve their constitutional right to unctuous statement, rank hypocrisy, and bitter diatribe. Whenever possible they presented their own interest as a synonym for "the will of the people," and certainly they were as swift as the Republicans to reverse their prior positions with respect to states' rights and the authority of the courts, but they seemed to know the difference between what was said and what was meant. More at ease in the company of their own cynicism, they didn't mistake their opponents for the friends of Darth Vadar or senior consultants to the Antichrist. Yes, politics was about the grasp for power, sometimes by any means available and often not a pretty sight, but where else did one find the weapons contract or the milk subsidy if not in the legislative game of three-card monte?

The Republican visionaries frown on ambiguity—as subjective and imperfect as a dimpled chad—and, like the long-lost legions of the 1960s counterculture, they imagine themselves bearers of a higher truth at odds with a world they never made. They belong to the party of transcendence, captivated by the beauty of ideological abstraction and contemptuous of low-born historical fact, always being confronted by monsters and apparitions instead of by the ordinary interests and desires of other human beings. The political zealots of the 1960s tended to appear on the ideological left, allied with the promise of a utopian future. The Republican risorgimento of the 1980s relocated the good news in the memory of an arcadian American past where John Wayne and Ronald Reagan rode together at the head of the wagon trains moving west into the California sunset. The scouts and trail bosses who served as Reagan's economic, spiritual, and foreign-policy advisers (many of them now attached to President Bush the Younger) haven't brooked the insult of a new idea in twenty years, which possibly is why I could never match the frenzied Republican commentary with the discussion of the election among people who weren't speaking to a camera.

Remarking on the turn of events in Florida over the span of five weeks with a fairly large number of people in New York and Washington (on the telephone, at dinner parties and subway stops, waiting in line at an airport or a movie theater), I seldom came across the rancorous tones of voice that showed up in the news media. Unless bound to party doctrine or the hope of appointment in a Bush or a Gore administration, the respondents stood willing to grant either candidate unclouded title to the White House. For the most part they saw the dispute as a political quarrel rather than as a constitutional crisis, and they didn't much care which of the two sides won the game of capture the flag. Their good humor I sometimes could attribute to their fair-mindedness and forbearance, at other times to a lack of interest in what's become of a national politics given over to politicians who fancy themselves as born-again aristocrats and biblical prophets. When listening to Trent Lott or reading the *Wall Street Journal,* I was reminded of Kenneth Starr looking for a scarlet letter somewhere on the person of Monica Lewinsky and the road-show Savonarolas in Congress crying down the wrath of Heaven on President Clinton's penis.

But then I remembered what I'd seen on the morning of December 9 at the public library in Tallahassee—judges and county officials doing their best to come up with an honest count and a fair judgment of the ballots ignored by a machine. They were keeping faith with the idea of the country's democratic institutions in the hands of a democratic people, and although mocked by Mr. Baker and ordered by the Supreme Court to cease and desist, they sifted through the boxes of computer cards as deliberately as if they were examining a mortgage contract, and I was proud of what I took to be their impartiality and seriousness of intent.

If my bias had been dormant on the morning of November 8, by December 12, when the Supreme Court ushered Mr. Bush into the White House, I could recognize it not as a preference for Al Gore and the Democrats but as opposition to the parties of transcendence and a fear of fools armed with the bright swords of shining ideology.

February 2001

Mirror, Mirror on the Wall

We've all had some bad times and some good times. But if you
believe in yourself and nuthin' else, your dreams will come
true . . . in the wishing well.
—Denise Rich

To watch President Clinton and his wife cash out of the
White House last winter was to watch two winning con-
testants collect their jackpot future on a network game
show—the happy couple beaming in the limelight, thrilled with
the $13 million in prize money presented by their book publish-
ers, excited about their holiday travel destinations (a Senate seat
for her, a New York office in the sky for him), pleased with the
home furnishings, the new golf clubs, the silver flatware and cash-
mere shawls. A wonderful American moment for Mom and Dad
and Chelsea and the dog, but where was the customary round of
spontaneous applause, and why no joyful clash of cymbals?

The studio audience failed to respond to the cue cards, and
somebody forgot to alert the band. Even as the Clintons were

exiting the stage, the news media took up the cudgels of rebuke, scolding the happy couple for their bad manners and deplorable taste, for the belated confession to the crime of perjury and the pardons distributed like Mardi Gras confetti to a crowd of cheering felons. Nor were the media content to let the matter drop. For nearly three weeks the columnists and editorial writers counted and recounted the cost of the items received from Denise Rich ($7,375 for tables and chairs, upwards of $450,000 for a presidential library), from Steven Spielberg (china soup tureen, $4,920), from Ken Burns (photograph of Duke Ellington, $800). When they weren't running the numbers the pastors in the newspaper pulpits recalled the sinful encounter with Monica Lewinsky, rummaged through their dictionaries for words strong enough to convey an image of unremitting selfishness and unsated greed— both Clintons likened to cormorants and stoats, natural-born catch basins, hollow as abandoned mines, eager to devour all the golf balls, every toasted almond, the last shred of gossip.

The more rabid tirades tended to appear in the media associated with the Republican Party and attitudes supposedly conservative—in *The Weekly Standard,* the *New York Post, National Review,* etc.—which seemed to me both spiteful and wrongheaded. The publications in question never tire of preaching the gospel of free-range capitalism; the American consumer society defined as the wonder of the world, the country founded on the fortune-bearing dreams of wealth and fame. Why then vilify the Clintons for following the instructions on the label? Who else more exuberantly personifies the buoyant spirit of the Miller beer commercials?

*   *   *

The media criticism proceeded from a premise known to Aristotle, and while the Clintons were carrying off the White House chairs, I came across a particularly lucid reformulation of it in David Selbourne's *The Principle of Duty*. First published in England in 1997, the book was reissued in January by the University of Notre Dame Press, and in the preface to the American edition the author sums up, in five pages, the whole of the indictment stuffed into a year's subscription to the *Wall Street Journal*. Define the pursuit of happiness so broadly as to embrace every wish in every wishing well, believe in "nuthin' else" except the wolfish self let loose in the free markets of duty-free desire, and the result is tyranny. Not the tyranny of the English crown that plagued the eighteenth-century American colonies with "swarms of Officers" sent hither "to harass our people, and eat out their substance," but the tyranny imposed "without let or hindrance" by the assertions of an infinite number of impatient demands variously defined as freedoms, rights, privileges, and self-realizations. When writing the Declaration of Independence Thomas Jefferson also had in mind a "just and solid republican government" held together by citizens who recognized their obligation to the common good and so agreed—in the interest of their own safety as well as that of the republic—to leave some of the wishes at the bottom of the well. The assumption doesn't make much sense to a society composed of citizens in name only, "ostensible citizens" united by little else except the possession of a credit card and a password to the Internet.

Selbourne doesn't pretend to the capture of a new idea, and in support of his observations he cites the dictum of Spinoza ("Citizens are not born, but made") as well as the authority of Cicero, Mazzini, Edmund Burke, and Tom Paine. The strength of the book rests in the clarity of its perception that no commonwealth or decent form of democratic government (no matter how heavily armed with cruise missiles and well equipped with tax exemptions) can defend itself against the raids of freebooting moral entrepreneurs and self-proclaimed kings. Burke put the proposition as follows: "Society cannot exist unless a controlling power upon will and appetite be placed somewhere, and the less of it there is within, the more there must be without." The statement speaks to the success of the American markets in cosmetics and prescription drugs as well as to the population of the nation's prisons.

During earlier periods of American history the governing and possessing classes understood that their commercial voyages required some sort of civic ballast in the hold. But the social orders founded first on the Protestant Church and then on the quasi-religious faith in democracy have given way to a managerial elite loyal to nothing other than its own ambition, and instead of a *res publica* for which the citizens feel affection, we have a government casino open to every minority interest and political subtext capable of hiring a suite of high-priced lobbyists.

To watch the Clintons feed is not a pretty sight, but rather than confront the spectacle of a disaggregated society unwilling to acknowledge a principle of duty, we talk about the loss of "leadership" or the failure of the nation's schools. No matter who happens to be making the speech—politician, cabdriver, university poet—all agree that only leadership can rescue the country from its stomach. Leadership and teaching the kids how to read.

The conversation never gets around to the truism that leaders can't exist without followers, that they depend upon a coherent governing class respectful of an ethical ideal that encompasses the particular duties of both the citizen and the state. The maintenance of such an ideal brings with it the burdens of moderation and restraint, which, if carried beyond the giving up of cigarettes and the third whiskey before dinner, seriously interfere with everybody's rights and self-realizations. The after-dinner speakers avoid the point. They prefer to speak of leadership as if it were a function of personality or an innate talent, like that for playing the piano or solving crossword puzzles, and when casting around for exemplary figures they mention surgeons, military commanders, and football coaches—specialists hired for special occasions. Nobody likes to dwell on the moral effort required of the audience as well as the stars of the show, and after the customary denunciations of Hollywood and the news media, the conversation drifts off into the mists of nostalgia. Long ago and once upon a time, America was famous for its leaders—handsome and stylish people who knew how to make sacrifices, ride horses, construct compound sentences.

The vague memory of film documentaries once seen on PBS or the History Channel provided George W. Bush with the whole of his platform in last year's election campaign. His admirers presented him as the candidate from 1955, an honorary member of

Tom Brokaw's "Greatest Generation," outfitted at birth with the civic virtues that carried his father through to victory in the Second World War. Here at last was a man of breeding, not known for his intelligence or close acquaintance with the affairs of state but somebody who could be relied upon not to steal the spoons. The speechwriters made free use of the words "civility" and "honor," and what they had in mind was a trip down memory lane with Private Ryan and General Reagan. Vote Republican, and return with George W. Bush to the America of yesteryear.

Within the provinces coded red on November's electoral map, so poignant was the sentiment in favor of a social order rooted in the ground of moral principle that the candidate could as easily have been made of wood—a wagon wheel that once had rolled west on the Oregon Trail, Ty Cobb's baseball bat, a post from the Yale fence. It didn't matter what the totem said or didn't say; the mere fact of its presence on the White House lawn was certain to please the ancestors and reawaken the Great Spirit of Abraham Lincoln. The promotion moved the merchandise, and the new President's Cabinet appointments argued for the restoration of the picture-postcard past:

- The attorney general, John Ashcroft, secure in the attitudes current on the Missouri frontier in 1851—firm in the belief that Negroes couldn't be trusted with the vote and seeing nothing morally amiss with the Confederate defense of slavery, wary of any freedoms too recklessly granted to women, approving the occasional but judicious resort to gunplay, informing an audience at Bob Jones

University in 1999 that in America "we have no King but Jesus."

- Gale A. Norton, secretary of the interior, inclined to look upon the public lands in a way that would have been familiar to John C. Frémont and Colonel George A. Custer—a hostile wilderness meant to be improved by cattle ranchers and timber merchants, by mining companies, itinerant evangelists, and the United States Cavalry.

- Donald Rumsfeld, secretary of defense, still engaged in the Cold War with the ghosts of the Soviet empire, brooding over maps of the artillery positions on the Kamchatka Peninsula, drawing up blueprints for an invincible missile shield sure to protect San Diego and St. Louis from nuclear annihilation.

Thus supported by the certainties of the near and distant past, the Bush Administration during its first weeks in office moved to reverse the flow of time. No more money for misguided charities apt to mention the word "abortion" to strange women in foreign lands; a new White House Office of Faith-Based and Community Initiatives through which the government would disburse funds to its unfortunate citizens in return for their enlistment in the army of God; a restructuring of the tax laws that rewarded the industry of the deserving rich and punished the indolence of the unworthy poor.

The nineteenth-century moral prescriptions presumed the existence of a citizenry willing to take the medicine, but in the year

2001, where does President Bush find a constituency loyal to a civic order grounded on a premise that doesn't translate into the question "What's in it for me?" When George Marshall retired as secretary of state in 1949, every important New York publisher offered him large sums of money to write his memoirs. Marshall declined the invitations to wealth and the lecture circuit. No, he said in effect, I did nothing other than my duty as a citizen; the correspondence and the state papers belong to the United States, and when I walk out of this office, I'm taking nothing with me except my hat.

Who among the company of our contemporary "leaders" would not leave the hat and take the files? Let them for a moment lose focus on the great and noble art of self-promotion, and somebody might steal from them a crumb of profit or a scrap of patronage.

During the second of last year's presidential debates Vice President Al Gore testified to the sincerity of Governor Bush's emotions—"I believe his statement that he has a good heart"— and I see no reason to doubt the certification. Nor do I see why it matters. We're talking about a President appointed by five Supreme Court justices who evinced as little respect for the law as Bill and Hillary Clinton. Bush's election campaign raised $193 million, the largest sum invested in prospective government favors in the history of the country. The President's principal advisers represent the private rather than the public interest, men trained and cosseted by the corporations, accustomed to plundering the landscape and the U.S. Treasury on behalf of the oil and defense industries. I don't think we can

expect them to begin taking to heart the maxims of Marcus
Aurelius.

The Republicans in Washington over the last thirty years have
proved themselves as swinish in their habits as the Democrats,
eating out the people's substance at the troughs of entitlement
and graft, bidding up the price of their memoirs to the same
publishers in the market for news of Monica Lewinsky's underwear. No fewer than 138 of President Ronald Reagan's government appointees found themselves either investigated for official
misconduct or charged with violations of the criminal code. The
savings-and-loan swindle of the middle 1980s that cost the American taxpayers $500 billion was best understood as a deft robbery
rather than a failed economic policy. President Reagan's trading
of arms for hostages in Iran established the precedent for Marc
Rich's business practice in the same country, and the pardon
granted by President Bush I to Caspar Weinberger, the secretary
of defense, for his assistance in the deal was as much a travesty of
justice as the pardon granted by President Clinton to the husband
of his favorite songwriter. Nor were the Republicans shy about
receiving gifts. Nancy Reagan departed the White House with
shoes and dresses worth $1 million, the elder Bush with a collec-
tion of custom-made fishing rods a good deal more expensive than
Clinton's golf clubs.

Why then so much frothing at the mouth when Bill and Hillary went off into the golden sunset with the coffee tables and the

lamps? Possibly because so many critics, among them the most vociferous, don't enjoy looking at themselves in a mirror. In the faces of President and Mrs. Clinton they see, all too clearly, the fraudulence of their own claims to high-minded truth and noble virtue.

Because the United States no longer possesses a governing class licensed with the authority to issue the warrants of moral character and spiritual worth, we have instead a careerist elite, makeshift and provisional, manufactured at the expensive universities and programmed to flatter the whims of money, attend meetings, juggle budgets and policy decisions, write editorials for Rupert Murdoch's *Weekly Standard*. It is a timid and anxious crowd, gathering merit badges as avidly as Bill and Hillary and as glad to swallow the humiliations served with the caviar, the foundation grant, the tenured appointment, the smoked salmon, the promotion to the national news desk, and the weekend in the Hamptons. People groomed as culture bearers (very tasteful, very well behaved) don't like to think of themselves as mountebanks dancing for coins on a network game show, don't wish to see and hear the workings of their own digestive tracts.

April 2001

Model Citizens

When a prince's personal conduct is correct, his government is
effective without the issuing of orders. If his personal conduct is
not correct, he may issue orders, but they will not be followed.
                                        —CONFUCIUS

Mayor Rudolph Giuliani seldom misses a chance to
cleanse New York of its moral and spiritual impurities, and so it came as no surprise earlier this spring
when he appointed a board of examiners to vouch for the appro-
priateness of the art objects carried into museums dependent on
the grace and favor of the city budget. The naming of a Cultural
Affairs Advisory Commission to uphold "standards of decency"
followed from the mayor's disapproval of an exhibition mounted
in February by the Brooklyn Museum of Art that included a
photograph—fifteen feet long and three feet high—of a nude
black woman (the photographer herself) posed as the figure of
Christ at the Last Supper. Without taking the trouble to go to
Brooklyn, the mayor pronounced the photograph "outrageous" and

"disgusting," and to the newspaper reporters assembled at City Hall
he declared his intention "to look at what penalties are available
for this." When it was pointed out that he had failed in a previous
attempt to punish the same museum for its display in 1999 of a
painting of the Virgin Mary augmented with dried elephant dung,
the mayor said that his lawyers would be investigating "a way to
get this dispute to the place where I think we could win it, which
would be the Supreme Court of the United States."

No satisfactory judgment having arrived from Washington by
April 3, the mayor again summoned the press to City Hall to
introduce the twenty citizens, fifteen men and five women un-
blemished by postmodern aesthetic theory, to whom he had entrusted a task that he was careful not to define. Presumably the
commissioners were to act in the capacity of customs officials,
protecting the frontiers of established taste against the traffic in
subversive images, but they were as reluctant as the mayor to
discuss the regulations under which they would grant or deny an
import license. They contented themselves with looking upright
and respectable, decency their watchword, civility their lifelong
avocation, among them a rabbi, an imam, the mayor's divorce
lawyer, and a portrait painter known for his flattering likenesses
of corporate chief executives.

The news media's response to Giuliani's proclamation fluctu-
ated between mockery and alarm. The wits rejoiced in the ab-
surdist humor of high-toned moral statements handed down by a
mayor who liked to dress up in women's clothes and who accom-
modated both his current and former mistress with allowances
from the city treasury, and whose wife, estranged but still resident

in Gracie Mansion, showed up last fall in an off-Broadway theater performing a star turn in *The Vagina Monologues*. The more solemn critics mentioned Nazi Germany and worried about "the chilling effect" apt to dampen a museum director's enthusiasm for one of Benozzo Gozzoli's pictures of a mutilated saint.

For my own part I wondered why Giuliani continues to harass museums. Together with every other resident of New York, I know the mayor to be a very watchful man, suspicious of people speaking out of turn or without a Parks Department permit, quick to issue writs of prohibition against strip-club dancers, street vendors, minstrels, squeegee men, jaywalkers, and stray dogs. But why museums? Where was the imminent threat and what the present danger? No artist has menaced American society for forty years. Neither has any author, sculptor, or composer of string quartets. The contemporary audience prefers to take its cue from Benjamin Franklin in eighteenth-century Philadelphia, who observed that in the new republic "one schoolmaster is worth a dozen poets, and the invention of a machine or the improvement of an implement is of more importance than a masterpiece of Raphael," and the celebrity crowd before which Mayor Giuliani sometimes appears in fishnet stockings and high-heel shoes prefers objects that move and do things to those that merely wait to be understood, more interested in what Van Gogh's crazed hand did to his ear than in what his incomparable eye saw in the sunlight at Arles.

Most of the citizens likely to wander into the Brooklyn Museum on rainy weekend afternoons bring with them a sensibility trained by the entertainment media to appreciate the manufacture of art as a frivolous or domestic pursuit—an occupation comparable to weaving baskets or making jam. Safely classified as luxuries or toys and comprising any and all activities believed to be "creative," the line of goods known as "the arts" serves as a palliative to send to slums, children's hospitals, and Native American reservations; as a cure for boredom or drug addiction; as gifts of political patronage; or as any hobby, craft, or harmless amusement that keeps people off the streets. So easy is the democratic approach to Parnassus that more than 2 million Americans last year listed their occupation as "artist." Under the circumstances and not surprisingly, Mayor Giuliani construes artistic expression as a form of personal behavior and doesn't find much difference between the painter and the squeegee man, the ugly blot within the gilded frame as much an insult and an effrontery as the unwanted soap on the windshield of the Lexus.

Similarly in Washington this spring, the Republican majorities in command of Congress drew a distinction as careful as Mayor Giuliani's between the rights reserved to property and those grudgingly distributed to people. The legislation introduced or passed during the first 100 days of the Bush Administration (the tax bill; the boons granted to the banks; the easements awarded to the oil, mining, and insurance companies; etc.) reserves the freedom of expression to corporations and imposes on the citizenry the burdens of restraint. The Federal Communications Commission on April 6 affirmed its right to judge the decency or indecency of radio and television broadcasts, the ruling to be made in the interest of shielding children from depiction or description of "sexual or excretory organs or activities" in a "patently offensive" manner; ten days later the FCC indicated that it would remove the restraints that for the last twenty-six years had prevented television networks from combining with one another in the baroque art forms of sublime monopoly.

The lessons posted on the bulletin boards in Washington were as plain as Mayor Giuliani's order forbidding assembly of more than fifty persons on the steps of City Hall. Property is beautiful and must be sheltered from the rain; mere human beings, by nature unstable and rebellious, must be placed under strict surveillance and control. Heavy concentrations of large capital remain at liberty to do as they please—poison rivers, cut down forests, charge cruel rates of interest, experiment with lethal chemicals, deny medical care, eliminate species, repudiate debts, live handsomely beyond their incomes. Unincorporated individuals wait for instructions about where and when they can sing and dance. When not going off to prison for the possession of a single joint of marijuana, they submit to the censorship of their careless and ill-kempt speech—twenty-three employees dismissed by the *New York Times* for passing salacious email; the city of San Diego forbidding the use of the word "minority"; public schools everywhere in the country proscribing books that children must not read.

Let any criticism be brought against a society so obviously just, and the fault invariably will be found in the character of individuals, never in the arrangement of the political or economic furniture. The public scolds pointing to the proofs of moral degeneration and cultural decay assign the blame to behaviors deemed "permissive and destructive"—to high school students cheating on their term papers and indolent auto mechanics cheating on their wives, to Internet pornographers dispensing images of sex and violence, to vicious rap singers, predatory lesbians, and the poor example set by President Clinton, a libertine so promiscuous in his habits that the Republican managers of his impeachment trial compared him to a bad smell.

The latter-day Savonarolas ground their programs of reform on the premise of "accountability," but accountability is not a word that applies to property; accountability is "personal," usually a matter of poor work habits, a lack of dignity, the failure to acquire sentiments appropriate to museums under the guidance of wise counselors upholding "standards of decency." Money doesn't smell, and the charges of "permissive and destructive" behavior don't accrue to the accounts of corporations. The man or woman attempting to light a cigarette in a California restaurant stands accused of a crime against humanity; the factory that paints the Indiana sky with coal smoke contributes to the patriotic sum of the gross national product. An after-dinner speaker who criticizes a book by a Jewish author or an aria sung by an Italian tenor finds himself condemned as a "racist"; the advertising agency that tells a fetching lie about a hairspray or a hamburger wins a prize for inventive adjectives. The film director who decorates her movie in the colors of freak-show sensuality becomes the subject for a diatribe by William Bennett or an outraged editorial in the *Wall Street Journal*; the production studio receives the gratitude of the stockholders for selling the value-added content into the Asian and European markets. Mayor Giuliani declares obnoxious a clichéd photograph in an obscure art exhibition, and when, during the same week in Manhattan, one of the Disney companies opens the garishly advertised movie *Blow* as a tribute to the romance of the cocaine trade and a *Festspiel* of soft pornography, the mayor utters not even a mild bleat of small objection.

Like the mayor behind the frowning mask of Christian conscience, the government in Washington runs the con man's game of bait and switch. The defenders of the nation's welfare direct the shows of moral force against forms of expression in no way threatening to the public health and safety; simultaneously, and with only a brief pause of rhetorical qualm or hesitation, they subsidize the standard business practices that inflict the damage they so piously deplore. Secure in the support of a compliant and applauding press, they rely on the museum-going public to understand that it is the successful businessman, acting with perfect and enlightened selfishness, who sets the standard of civic virtue and generates the golden store of wealth that makes fruitful the garden of the American dream. The jaywalkers and the squeegee men should tip their hats and remember to be grateful. The well-ordered state is synonymous with the well-managed retail outlet, and if the sales and shipping clerks faithfully complete their tasks (good work habits, dignified deportment, sentiments appropriate to all occasions) maybe one day they, too, will become billionaire CEOs and so step up to glory.

The media never tire of promoting the joys of oligarchy and the privileges of wealth. It doesn't matter whether stock-market prices rise or fall, or how many Internet companies sink into the sloughs of bankruptcy, the newsstands every week bloom with brilliant images of the capitalist Olympus—the captains of corporate finance elevated to the pantheon of Roman gods, posed in the frames of expensive real estate, attended by nymphs and comforted with grapes, circling the narrow earth in Boeing 737's inlaid with sandalwood and ivory, intervening in the affairs of mortal men in the manner of Neptune playing with the sea.

Forty years ago in the United States the word "public" served as a synonym for selfless dedication to the common good (public servant, public health, public interest) and the word "private" carried with it the suggestion of selfish greed (private interest, private bank, private railroad car). Two generations of sustained economic prosperity have reversed the political usages of the words. "Public" connotes waste, poverty, incompetence, and fraud; "private" connotes honesty, intelligence, efficiency, and noble purpose.

In line with the privatization of our schools, hospitals, and prisons, we apparently wish to privatize the little that remains of what used to be called the public square. Ballparks and convention centers bear the names of telephone and airline companies; athletes wear the insignia of their corporate sponsors; the Boston subway system offers to sell the naming rights to four of its busiest and most historic stations, among them Back Bay and Downtown Crossing, to any business enterprise willing to pay an annual fee somewhere in the decent vicinity of $2 million. New York City rents its uniformed police officers ($27 an hour plus handling charges) to any uptown optimate seeking to provide a private dance or dinner party with an atmosphere of stately and reassuring calm. The officers come complete with bulletproof vests and the powers of arrest; the client pays for the liability insurance that covers the cost of lawsuits arising from complaints about the deployment of excessive force. Another five years, and we can expect to see the national parks named for the manufacturers of heavy automobiles and light beer.

As with the country's sports arenas and public parks, the public discourse once thought to be synonymous with the workings of democracy now presents itself in forums draped with corporate trademarks. The citizen who wishes to make a political speech must first adjust his text to the private definitions of commercial speech. Any citizen refusing the choice of mouthwashes and breath fresheners remains free to post his or her dissenting opinion on a website somewhere in the Australian outback of the Internet.

The critics who decry Mayor Giuliani's scourging of the Brooklyn Museum take the wrong lesson from the tale. Let them learn not from his precept but by his example and so transfer their sense of right and wrong from the private to the public sector. If the Supreme Court can construe the Fourteenth Amendment to the Constitution in such a way that it endows the corporation with the rights and attributes of a person, why should a person not aspire to the condition of a corporation? What wonders of personal self-realization might not follow from so marvelous a virgin birth? Bound by law to no purpose other than its own profit, untroubled by the nuisance of a conscience, and its sphere of moral reference reduced to that of a flatworm or a fern, the corporation feels not the sting of envy, the pang of hunger, the fear of death. Distribute the same freedoms of movement and expression to the American people as a whole—allowing them to spin off their mistakes and disappointing progeny as nonperforming assets, to repudiate their debts and live handsomely beyond their means—and we all might enter into the dream of heaven favored by the nation's leading politicians and sold in the nation's better stores.

June 2001

The Boys Next Door

But that was in another country, and besides, the wench is dead.
　　　　　　　　　　—CHRISTOPHER MARLOWE

*J*ust as NBC during the last years of the Clinton Administration refurbished the morally threadbare White House
with the comforts of *The West Wing,* CBS next autumn
will present *The Agency,* a prime-time dramatic series intended to
repair and improve the public understanding of the CIA. The
producers set themselves an ambitious task. The Agency's reputation for chronic stupidity and criminal incompetence is long
established and well deserved. Taken unawares by the outbreak of
the Korean War in 1950 and by the Soviet invasion of Hungary
in 1956, the Agency wrongly assessed (or falsely estimated) the
strength and resolve of the enemy during the entire twenty years
of the Vietnam War, was surprised by the Islamic revolution in
Iran in 1978, not only failed to anticipate but also refused to

acknowledge the collapse of the Soviet Union's Communist empire in 1989. When not making mistakes with its map overlays and geopolitical analysis, the Agency for the last fifty years has busied itself with lying to the United States Congress, practicing the sport of political assassination, running surveillance on 1.5 million American citizens deemed subversive and/or undesirable, embracing the joys of paranoid fantasy and imbecile conspiracy theory. All in all as impressive an exhibit of bureaucratic rubble and intellectual decay as exists anywhere in the city of Washington, and thus a project demanding every measure of the image-maker's art to furnish it with the consolations of virtual reality.

Preliminary filming began last April at CIA headquarters in Langley, Virginia, and, judging by the report in the *New York Times,* it took place in an atmosphere as sunny and warm as a Boy Scout picnic. The paper's correspondent remarked on the enthusiastic spirit of collaboration—the director setting up location shots of the building and grounds, low-ranking CIA operatives (among them "a fresh-faced twenty-nine-year-old woman with long black hair, dressed in a well-cut black suit") happy to play their parts as extras, actors walking briskly back and forth through the security checkpoints, the technical crew granted clearance to the gift shop to buy baseball caps embroidered with the Agency's insignia, the cameras moving around under the supervision of Chase Brandon, the public-affairs officer in charge of distributing the propaganda. Presented as a smiling man on whose authority a reader could rely, Brandon was quoted as saying: "This is such a different place than what it used to be. We've got a store and a fine arts commission and a museum. We've really become more, well, normal in our daily course of events as we continue to remain what we are, a secret intelligence organization helping policy makers and military planners carry out their mission."

The *Times* reporter noticed nothing in the statement or the scene conducive to the tone of irony; neither did the several journalists in New York to whom I mentioned the filming as a virtuoso performance in the theater of the absurd. They thought the joke was old, at least ten years behind the times. Maybe as late as 1990 a few colleges still prohibited the CIA's recruitment of students on their campuses, and the Agency's misadventures in Nicaragua and Iran were still fresh enough in the public mind to warrant suspicion of both its character and its motives. The discovery of a Soviet mole under the lawn at Langley in 1994 led to congressional investigations in both the Senate and the House, and after listening to the testimony about how Aldrich Ames for nine years had been selling important American secrets to Moscow without arousing the least suspicion among his colleagues— despite Ames's heavy drinking and sudden possession of inexplicably large sums of money—the politicians briefly considered dismantling the Agency.

But that was then, and this was now, and hadn't I noticed that the best opinion in Washington favored the notion of the United States dressed up in the costume of the Roman Empire? What else did I expect? A proper empire requires the presence of barbarians on the frontiers, and as proof of the need for fanciful weapons programs, the Bush Administration was promoting a revival of the atmospherics of the Cold War. Let the United States once again be threatened by monstrous enemies—rogue states, starving mobs, Arab terrorists, deadly chemicals, treacherous Chinese—and the prime-time television audience deserves to know that standing watch on the ramparts of freedom we have a lot more people in this country as steadfast as Allison Janney and Martin Sheen.

Long ago and in another country, I could have written an appropriately swell and heartwarming script. In the autumn of 1957, a year out of college and recently returned to the United States after several months in Europe, I applied for work at the *Washington Post,* the White House, and the CIA. Dwight Eisenhower was president, the Communist hordes were at the gates of Western Europe, and the murderous farce in Vietnam hadn't yet divided the country into camps of opposing virtue. The Cold War offered the promise of high adventure, and the nation's newly commissioned intelligence service attracted idealistic young men eager to leave at once, preferably at night and under an assumed name, on the next train for Berlin.

The written and physical examinations occupied the better part of a week, and then, after a discreet interval of administrative silence, I was summoned to an interview with five operatives in their late twenties, all of them graduates of Yale and not unlike President George W. Bush in their appearance and manner. The interview took place in one of the Quonset huts near the Lincoln Memorial that had served as the Agency's temporary headquarters during World War II. The military design of a building hastily assembled for an urgent purpose imparted an air of understated glory, an effect consciously reflected in the studied carelessness of the young men asking the questions. Very pleased with themselves but trying not to be too obvious about it, they exchanged knowing references to "that damned thing in Laos" and allowed me to understand that we were talking about the Varsity Team, the Big Game, the Right Stuff.

Prepared for nothing less, I had spent the days prior to the interview memorizing the events of the Bolshevik Revolution, the sequence of the Hapsburg emperors, the geography of Alsace-Lorraine. None of the study was of any use. Instead of being encouraged to discuss the treaties of Brest-Litovsk or name the four roads through the forest of the Ardennes, I was asked three questions bearing on my social qualifications for admission into what the young men across the table clearly regarded as the best fraternity on the campus of the freedom-loving world:

1. When standing on the thirteenth tee at the National Golf Links in Southampton, which club does one take from the bag?

2. On sailing into Hay Harbor on Fishers Island, what is the direction of the prevailing wind?

3. Does Muffy Hamilton wear a slip?

The first and second questions I answered correctly, but Muffy Hamilton I knew only at a distance. In the middle 1950s she was a glamorous figure on the Ivy League weekend circuit, very beautiful and very rich, much admired for the indiscriminate fervor of her sexual enthusiasms. At Williams on a winter weekend I had seen her dancing on a table, and once upon a time at the Fence Club in New Haven I had handed her a bottle of brandy with a glass of milk. About the mysteries of her underwear my knowledge was secondhand, my sources compromised, my information limited to a rumor of Belgian lace.

The three questions, however, put an end to my interest in the CIA. The complacence of my examiners was as smooth as their matching silk handkerchiefs and ties, and when I excused myself from the rest of the interview (apologizing for having misread the job description and wasted everybody's time) I remember being frightened by the presence of so much self-congratulation crowded into so small a room. As arrogant as they were vain, invincibly certain of their moral and intellectual primogeniture, the members of the credentials committee ordained by God and Yale basked in the sun of omniscience, and from that day forward I've never questioned the Agency's talent for making a mess of almost any operation that it condescended to undertake. Nor have I been surprised by the Agency's buffoonery and vindictiveness. Once disabused of the dream of power, nobody becomes more spiteful than the boy next door jilted by the beautiful Asian girl to whom he has given the beach house at Cam Ranh Bay, $100 million in helicopters, and God knows how many tons of high explosive.

The first few seasons of derring-do gave everybody reason to believe that the game might prove to be exciting, successful, and fun. Congress voted abundant supplies of money for which it demanded no accounting, and foreign agents in the 1950s sold at

bargain prices, sometimes for as little as a bar of chocolate or a
carton of cigarettes. The Agency recruited émigré armies to re-
capture the lost kingdoms of Poland, Bulgaria, and the Ukraine;
assisted with the removal of governments thought to be inconvenient in Iran, Guatemala, and the Philippines; conducted experiments (in Asia and Latin America) with the trade crafts of
extortion, bribery, and torture.

Within a very few years the victories proved to be illusory, or,
at best, ambiguous. Advance scouts for the émigré armies para-
chuted into the Slavic darkness and were never seen or heard from
again. By overthrowing the popular but socialist regime in Iran
(at the behest of the Anglo-Iranian Oil Company) the United
States opened the way first to the repressive tyranny of the Shah
of Shahs and then to the revolutionary zeal of the Ayatollah Khomeini. The forced departure of Jacobo Arbenz from Guatemala
(because his form of democratic socialism offended the United
Fruit Company) allowed for the arrival of a notably vicious military junta, and in the Philippines the outfitting of Ramón Mag-
saysay with anti-Communist propaganda served as prelude to the
corrupt regime of Ferdinand Marcos.

Nothing in the public record suggests that the Agency during
the last thirty-odd years has picked up on the news that the Statue
of Liberty cannot be made to stand on the pedestal of criminal
violence. The patrol boats sink, the guerrillas get lost in the
mountains, somebody blows up the bus terminal instead of the
radio station. Consider the bungled invasion at the Bay of Pigs,
where, without the least hint of a plausible reason, the CIA expected a crowd of Cuban peasants to rise from the sugarcane and

march gloriously to Havana while singing Broadway show tunes. Marvel at the subtlety of the Agency's plot to remove Sukarno as the president of Indonesia—by releasing to theater audiences in Jakarta a propaganda film entitled *Happy Days* that purportedly showed Sukarno (played by a Mexican actor wearing a mask) in bed with a Soviet agent (played by a California actress wearing a wig). Dwell briefly on the comedy of what in 1986–87 was billed as the Iran/Contra affair—the Agency thinking to sell an arms-for-hostages deal to the mullahs in Teheran by offering the gifts of a Bible and a cake, depositing $10 million in the wrong Swiss bank account, hiring drunken aircraft mechanics in El Salvador, and dropping munitions into the wrong jungles in Nicaragua. Pass lightly over the fact that prior to the Gulf War in 1991 the Agency confidently informed the Pentagon that Saddam Hussein meant to attack Saudi Arabia, not Kuwait.

But as demonstrated most recently by the Agency's accidental targeting of the Chinese Embassy in Belgrade (i.e., "helping policy makers and military planners carry out their mission"), the boys next door learn nothing from their mistakes. Their vanity remains handsomely intact, and so does their hope of solving, maybe this year or next in the mountains of Colombia, the mysteries of cocaine smuggling, money laundering, and Muffy Hamilton's underwear. Although I can understand how it might be possible to admire their persistence, I don't know why we continue to give them money, and when I notice that in the current fiscal year the Agency has submitted a budget request for $30 billion, I remember that in John le Carré's novel *Tinker, Tailor, Soldier, Spy,* an old connoisseur of the world's secrets tells an apprentice espionage agent that their best information—acquired at large expense and with heavy loss of human life—is probably false. The ancient spy poses his judgment as a question: "Ever bought a fake picture, Toby? The more you pay for it, the less inclined you are to doubt its authenticity."

An agent in the British Foreign Service before becoming a novelist, le Carré understood that covert actions usually took place at the not-very-important margins of not-very-important events, and that when extended over a period of more than four days they hide nothing from anybody except the people paying the bills. He also understood that the "magic formulae and hocus-pocus of the spy world" recommend themselves to "declining powers," to men and institutions losing their strength and becoming fearful of shadows. "When the king is dying," he said, "the charlatans rush in."

So do the soap-opera stars, the makeup artists, the sound crews wearing embroidered baseball caps. The *Times* correspondent introduced them as people who had come to help, happy to tell uplifting stories and not inclined to sarcasm. Michael Beckner, the principal writer for the series, described it in almost the same words as those deployed by Chase Brandon—"less *Mission Impossible* and more about the families and lifestyles and personal day to day lives of the men and women of the CIA." The remark suggests that we can rely on CBS to make sure that every covert operation and all the secondary plots work the way they are supposed to work—each week before the last commercial a bomb defused, a terrorist captured, a city rescued from bubonic plague. But more importantly, in the foreground of the episode we'll meet the fragile human beings (single mothers, caring fathers, recovering alcoholics, etc.) going about their daily rounds between the gift shop and the pistol range, and as we learn to love them all, each and every one, we'll come to know that America is defended, if not in fact at least in fiction, by an engagingly dysfunctional family of patriots who remain capable (despite the distractions of lost dogs and extramarital love affairs) of reading a satellite photograph and finding their way through Bulgarian customs.

The producers can expect the critics to be kind; certainly they can trust the network to inject promotional spots into the news broadcasts prepared for Dan Rather and Mike Wallace. Change a few names on the TelePrompTer—last week in Kabul instead of this week in Dar es Salaam—and the two reels of virtual reality become reassuringly indistinguishable. Whether packaged as news or entertainment, the sale and distribution of government propaganda no longer provoke quibbles of dissent. The official spokesmen hand out the press releases; the baseball caps from NBC and CBS wrap them up in cellophane as good-luck charms meant to ward off evil spirits shrieking in a foreign wind.

July 2001

The American Rome

On the Theory of Virtuous Empire

> Innocence is like a dumb leper who has lost his bell, wandering
> the world, meaning no harm.
> —GRAHAM GREENE

When the United States in early May lost its seat on the United Nations' Human Rights Commission in Geneva, the immediate response in New York and Washington was one of genuine astonishment. Important people looked questioningly at their cell phones and didn't know whether they'd heard a false rumor or a foolish joke. How could such things be, and where had reason fled? Surely it was well known that America had invented human rights, forever coming to the rescue of lost children and failed democracies. Never before in the fifty-four years of the commission's existence had the United States been excluded from the committee rooms of conscience; never in living memory had the "world's only superpower" suffered so undeserved a mockery at the hands of its ungrateful dependents.

The offending gesture, an organizational vote within the U.N. Economic and Social Council, took place on a Thursday in Switzerland, and by nightfall on the nearer shore of the Atlantic a hastily assembled quorum of gold-plated American opinion (prominent journalists, responsible politicians, dependable historians) was hurrying into print or a television studio with the offers of an explanation. For the most part they resembled late-Victorian British admirals on loan from an operetta by Gilbert and Sullivan. Thirty seconds into the broadcast or two paragraphs down the page the initial expressions of disbelief swelled into an uproar of heavy sarcasms, dark frowns, indignant manifestations of injured vanity, wounded virtue, baffled omnipotence. Was there no limit to the world's effrontery and gall? Were these people imbeciles or merely impertinent? Had they forgotten that they owed their freedom to sit around talking nonsense in overpriced restaurants to America's benevolence, America's money, America's air force?

The admirals were accustomed to insults from the Algerians and Fidel Castro, but what they found incomprehensible was the treachery of the European plenipotentiaries who were supposed to be our friends. The commission every year realigns its membership in such a way that the bloc of Western democracies receives three of the open seats, one of them customarily reserved to the United States if the United States comes up for reelection. But this year something went wrong with the divine right of kings, and when the secret ballot was counted the United States had received only twenty-nine of fifty-three possible votes, as opposed to fifty-two for France, forty-one for Austria, thirty-two for Sweden. Prior to

the voting no fewer than forty-three countries had provided Secretary of State Colin Powell with written assurances of their support. The result reduced fourteen of the letters to worthless scraps
of paper, which was preposterous, unspeakable, not to be borne. I
didn't watch all the Washington talk shows or read all the newspaper commentaries, but those that I did see didn't offer much
variation in tone and theme:

"**TYRANTS TAKE OVER**"—Headline in the *Wall Street
Journal* over an editorial making the point that the United
States had been expelled from a commission that welcomed
among its members representatives from Libya, Sudan, and
Syria—i.e., countries not known to cherish a concern for
human rights.

"**Thugs' club . . . a sewer of brutality and repression**"—
Characterization of the Human Rights Commission in a *New
York Post* editorial suggesting that the U.N. be voted off the
island of Manhattan.

"**Sneak diplomatic attack**"—William Safire in the *New
York Times* explaining the U.N. vote as a plot "led by Communist China and Communist Cuba, and with the conniv-
ance of French diplomats currying favor with African and
Arab dictators"; the purpose of the plot revealed as an attempt by a backstabbing "pack of hypocrites" to punish the
United States for taking the side of Israel in "the war started
by order of Yasir Arafat."

"New period of official anti-Americanism"—Michael
Kelly in the *Washington Post* attributing America's loss of its
seat on the commission to the envy and resentment of the
European members, "because Europe's ruling classes will
never forgive us for constructing a world in which they no
longer rule over anything except artisan cheeses."

Amidst the hectic waving of flags a few bystanders (some journalists, not many politicians) observed that the rebuff in Geneva
wasn't entirely unwarranted. The United States over the last several years has been slow to pay its U.N. dues (the account currently
$1.3 billion in arrears), and it stands opposed to a long list of
policy initiatives put forward in the name of human rights, among
them the Kyoto Protocol limiting emissions of carbon dioxide into
the earth's atmosphere and the treaty establishing an international
criminal court. Nor has the newly enskyed Republican oligarchy
in Washington shown much respect for what its drum majors in
Congress and the Pentagon disparage as "weak-kneed multilater-
alism." President Bush prefers the more manly acts of "unabashed
unilateralism," and during his first few months in office the American government bombed Baghdad, bullied the Russians, announced its intention to nullify the 1972 Anti-Ballistic Missile
Treaty, guaranteed the prospect of war in Asia if China fools
around with the sovereignty of Taiwan. Yes, it was possible that
some countries (the poorer countries certainly, even some European countries clinging to the memories of their former grandeur)
might have their reasons for objecting to the shows of American
resolve, and one could almost see (if one looked very closely and

imagined oneself as feckless as Italy or as obstinate as Germany) how it might be possible to misperceive America's fundamental goodness of heart.

As cautious as they were faint, the voices not raised in righteous anger didn't rate much space in the papers, and they were easily shouted down by the operatic chorus deploring the affront in early May in a tone consistent with Charles Krauthammer's trumpet solo in *Time* magazine in early March:

> America is no mere international citizen. It is the dominant power in the world, more dominant than any since Rome. Accordingly, America is in a position to re-shape norms, alter expectations and create new realities. How? By unapologetic and implacable demonstrations of will.

Although heartily endorsed by the Republican members of Congress, also by the kind of people who think the phrase "world's only superpower" is a Homeric epithet like "rosy-fingered dawn" or "wine-dark sea," the Time Inc. theory of the American Rome doesn't travel well. The topic was often in the conversation during a week in April when I was in Paris to talk to a French publisher, but the feeling of resentment was less apparent than a sense of disappointment. An author of enigmatic novels cited a recent poll of French public opinion that asked for "images that come to mind when you think of America." Presented with a short list of words applicable to the United States, a majority of the respondents chose synonyms for barbarism: "violence" (67 percent), "power" (66 percent), "inequality"

(49 percent), and "racism" (42 percent); only 20 percent mentioned "freedom," and 4 percent "generosity."

Not the same people who had come ashore on Omaha Beach
in June of 1944, and even a columnist from *Le Monde* wanted to
know what had become of the freedom-loving Americans of song
and story—woefully uncultured, of course, also vulgar and naive,
but generous to a fault and true to their faith in their fellow man?
The wits at the dinner tables on both banks of the Seine didn't
omit the customary hors d'oeuvres of scorn (President Bush described as "a ventriloquist's dummy," also as "the Forrest Gump
of American politics"), but where was the once-upon-a-time democratic republic, and why were they inclined to think of the
United States as a department store or a stomach, not as the embodiment of a courageous principle or an ennobling idea? Somewhere in the endgame of the Cold War the old citizen army
apparently had gotten lost, replaced by a generation of would-be
hegemons toying with the dream of empire. The rulers of artisan
cheeses didn't question the American wish to strike handsome
Roman poses in the togas of "the world's only superpower," but
they perceived a problem in logic. How did the inheritors of a
stupendous military and economic fortune mean to balance the
harsh imperatives of power against the softer claims of conscience?
Unlike the Americans, the ancient Romans didn't confuse the
conquering of distant provinces with the distribution of global
happiness, and where did the executives of Coca-Cola bottling
companies propose to find the moral and intellectual sangfroid to
manage civil unrest in Judaea, famine in Egypt, rebellion in Parthia and Leptis Minor?

The same questions were asked on four successive evenings, and gradually it occurred to me that the French didn't fully appreciate the doctrine of American innocence, what the first Puritans in the Massachusetts wilderness understood as their special appointment from Providence. Because God had chosen America as the construction site of the earthly Paradise, America's cause was always just and nothing was ever America's fault. Subsequent generations of American prophets and politicians have expressed the belief in different words—America, "The Last, Best Hope of Mankind"; America, "The Ark of Safety, The Anointed Civilizer"—but none of the witnesses ever fails to understand that whereas corrupt foreigners commit crimes against humanity, Americans cleanse the world of its impurities. We do so because we have a natural aptitude for the work and because without our humanitarian interventions (over Dresden and Hiroshima as well as at Château-Thierry and Iwo Jima) the whole scheme of creation might come loose in the wind and vanish in the night.

If every now and then an American commits a monstrous crime— Lee Harvey Oswald, Lt. William Calley, Timothy McVeigh—the action is declared un-American, senseless, unthinkable, so contrary to the laws of nature and the will of God that it can be intelligibly discussed only by senior churchmen and high-priced psychiatrists.[1] Never intrinsic to the American landscape or the American character, evil is a deadly and unlicensed import, an outlandish disease

---

[1]Students of America's special arrangement with Providence might find it useful to compare the punishment of Calley with that of McVeigh. Two terrorists, American born and trained, encouraged to regard the murder of civilians as a

smuggled through customs in a shipment of German philosophy or Asian rice. Innocent by definition, America invariably finds itself betrayed (at Pearl Harbor, the Little Big Horn, Havana Bay), and because we have been betrayed we always can justify the use of brutal or un-Christian means to defend the Ark of Safety against the world's treachery.

Which is why America never needs to appoint truth commissions similar to those established by South Africa, Chile, Burundi, and any other country seeking to come to terms with its inevitably tragic past. The American past isn't tragic. We are the children of revelation, not history, and together with the twice-born President Bush we can assume that because we possess a natural instinct for the good, we need not concern ourselves with law. Laws are for people unlucky enough to have been born without the DNA of virtue. Maybe Dick Cheney lacks the Emperor Nero's readiness to light a garden party with torches made from the still living remnants of 2,000 Christian slaves, but American B-52s can stack dead civilians like cordwood in the rubble of Hanoi, the pilots safe in the knowledge that they are doing what is right, their bombing runs bringing the good news that salvation is near at hand.

---

proper military objective. But Calley killed foreigners (102 Vietnamese peasants at My Lai in March 1968); he served three years of confinement to barracks at Fort Benning, Georgia. McVeigh, a veteran of the Gulf War, killed Americans (168 citizens in Oklahoma City in April 1995); he was portrayed by the news media as an incarnation of the devil, and the production costs of his trial and execution (i.e., the exorcism) amounted to $50 million.

No matter how often I explained the American rule of engagement that allowed for its blameless passage through the labyrinth of twentieth-century atrocity, I failed to persuade the French of the necessary distinction between ethnic and moral cleansing. When the other people at the table didn't scoff at the weakness of the reasoning, they charged me with cynicism or suspected an elaborate absurdity in imitation of Beckett or Céline.

A week later I returned to New York to find most of the eminent journalists in the city sprinkling incense on the news that Bob Kerrey—former senator from Nebraska, recipient of the Congressional Medal of Honor, voice of democratic conscience, president of The New School University in New York City—conceivably deserved to be reconfigured as a war criminal. The allegation took the form of a report published in the *New York Times Magazine* during the same week that the United Nations expelled the United States from the Human Rights Commission in Geneva, and the two events coming so close together in time coordinated the media's efforts to illuminate the doctrine of American grace.

The charge against Kerrey was backdated to the war in Vietnam. As a twenty-five-year-old lieutenant commanding a six-man team of Navy SEALs, Kerrey, in the Mekong Delta in February 1969, had led a raid on the hamlet of Thanh Phong that resulted in the killing of thirteen unarmed women and children. The after-action report didn't identify the dead as noncombatants, and Kerrey received a Bronze Star for an exploit deemed heroic. There the matter rested for nearly thirty years, until a *Newsweek* reporter, Gregory Vistica, came across some old military records, talked to the other members of the SEAL team, and approached Kerrey with the request for a clarification. When the story eventually appeared in print it was told in the voice of a consoling therapist rather than that of a reproving journalist. It wasn't that Vistica failed to state the facts—no enemy soldiers in the village, the peasants shot down like rabbits—but he weighted the sentiment in favor of Kerrey's torment, Kerrey's anguish, Kerrey tempted by the thought of suicide. Both in the magazine article and in the flurry of press interviews subsequent to its publication, the interest centered on the quality of Kerrey's remorse, the dead Vietnamese reduced to stage props backing up the soliloquies on the theme of innocence regained:

> "Now I can talk about it. It feels better already."
> "I have chosen to talk about it because it helps me to heal."
> "It's the shame. You can never . . . get away from it. It darkens your day."

Kerrey's serial acts of contrition evoked nods of warm and welcoming bathos almost everywhere in the media. Except for a few churlish remarks in *The Nation* and *The New Republic* (remarks to the effect that a war crime by any other name was still a war crime), the preservers of a nation's conscience were quick to recognize Kerrey as a victim of circumstance. A clean-limbed American youth sent on a terrorist errand in the dead of night and the fog of war. What else was a fellow to do? His commanding officer insisted on body counts and the collection of yellow ears. Surely Kerrey had suffered enough. Three weeks after the incident at Thanh Phong he had lost part of his right leg in the action at Cam Ranh Bay for which he received the Medal of Honor. Because a war hero cannot become a war criminal, the moral authorities on both the old left and the new right voted for acquittal, and the court of public opinion needed no more than a few days to find that the fault was in the war, not the warrior.

"That he felt remorse, that he sacrificed even more for his country . . . is enough for his salvation, and a harder task than most can imagine. That's a war hero, folks, a sinner redeemed by his sacrifice for a cause greater than his self-interest. That's Bob Kerrey, my friend and hero."—The judgment of Senator John McCain, handed down in an editorial for the *Arizona Republic*.

"It was dark, very dark."—David Halberstam, defending Kerrey's honor before an audience of New York intellectuals in Greenwich Village.

"It is hard for most of us to imagine the horrors of war. War is Hell. Traumatic events take place and their terrible effects may last a lifetime. We should all recognize the agony that Bob is going through and continues to deal with."—Statement from the Trustees of The New School University.

"For our country to blame the warrior instead of the war is among the worst and, regrettably, most frequent mistakes we, as a country, can make."—Joint press release issued by Senators Max Cleland (D., Ga.), Chuck Hagel (R., Nebr.), and John Kerry (D., Mass.), all of them veterans of the Vietnam War.

"To know or not to know? That is the political question." —Jim Hoagland, columnist in the *Washington Post.*

Hoagland didn't volunteer an answer, probably because his question was also a moral one, and when engaged in the ritual purification of the American soul it is always better to know as little as possible. The soft focus of blurred emotion is preferable to the unflattering clarities of thought or a distracting clutter of facts. George Bush Sr. reduced the operative principle to its simplest formulation when he was campaigning for the presidency in the summer of 1988. The U.S.S. *Vincennes,* an Aegis missile cruiser stationed in the Persian Gulf, shot down an Iranian airliner on July 3, under the mistaken impression that it was firing at a warplane. The error in judgment killed 290 civilian passengers en route to Dubai. Asked for a comment at a campaign stop in Washington, the candidate said, "I will never apologize for the United States. I don't care what the facts are."[2]

[2]Strong-minded hegemons think it demeaning to make apologies. When an American submarine rammed and sank a Japanese fishing trawler near Honolulu last February, drowning nine of the passengers onboard, Richard Cohen, a columnist for the *Washington Post,* complained about the excessive shows of sym-

Most of the exonerations of Kerrey also insisted on the point that he couldn't be fairly judged by anybody who hadn't done time in the free-fire zones of the Vietnamese hell. If you hadn't been there, you didn't know, and if you didn't know, you couldn't pass judgment. The syllogism offered the further advantage of reaffirming America's lack of responsibility for the whole of the Vietnam War. Some people had been there with Kerrey in the Mekong Delta; other people had been there with the generals in the Pentagon or with Presidents Lyndon Johnson and Richard Nixon in the White House; but nobody except God had been everywhere, and so, when you really got around to thinking about it, the war was God's fault. The bombing of Cambodia was a natural disaster, which was too bad for the Cambodians, but one of those things, like an African genocide or an earthquake in Honduras, that couldn't be helped.

The same cloud of incense and unknowing that descended on Kerrey's Bronze Star blots out the hope of public debate about what kind of country we think we have become. The media don't grant much of a hearing to bystanders who question the triumph of the

---

pathy on the part of the United States Navy. Reminding his readers that the accident occurred within sight of Pearl Harbor, he said, "This was Hawaii, for crying out loud. . . . So, one more time: we're sorry . . . of course we apologize for the loss of the *Ehime Maru* and the apparent deaths of nine persons aboard. But we are the same guys who have provided Japan with a security shield ever since World War II, helped rebuild a country and have been its steadfast ally and best friend. Don't make us sorry."

Pax Americana, and on most days of any week it's hard to open a newspaper or read a policy journal without submitting to a siege of imperial rhetoric. Thus, in the summer issue of *The National Interest*, none other than Henry Kissinger, filling in the basso continuo to Krauthammer's trumpet tune: "So long as the post–Cold War generation of national leaders is embarrassed to elaborate an unapologetic concept of enlightened national interest, it will achieve progressive paralysis, not moral elevation." Or again, in the same issue of *The National Interest,* Francis Fukuyama, former State Department official and author of *The End of History:* "A country that makes human rights a significant element of its foreign policy tends toward ineffectual moralizing at best, and unconstrained violence in pursuit of moral aims at worst."[3]

Transposed into the exchange of snappy sound bites on the Washington talk-show circuit, the theory of American empire becomes a complacent certainty. The pundits in residence compare notes with the visiting experts and find themselves in fond agreement on the great fact of America's colossal preeminence in the world—the size of its economy and the richness of its markets,

---

[3]Fukuyama doesn't mince his words, but Kissinger's sentence presumably makes better sense in German. Read in the context of Kissinger's policies in Asia and Latin America, the phrase "embarrassed to elaborate an unapologetic concept" probably can be taken to mean "unwilling to bribe, bomb, assassinate, or betray." The phrase "moral elevation" is more difficult. It's conceivable that the author imagines himself standing on a pile of corpses in Kurdistan, but then again, maybe he's thinking of himself as an equestrian statue on the White House lawn. In any event, a Roman pose, something to bring to mind the memory of noble Cicero.

the speed of its computers, the wonder of its weapons, the strength of its armies. Add to the sum of the superlatives the vast reach and sway of America's "soft power" (the T-shirts and the action movies, the cheeseburgers and the popular songs) and what we are talking about—as George just said, and as even Sam and Cokie will admit—is an empire on which—we might as well be blunt about it—the sun never sets. All present nod and chuckle, and the conversation proceeds to the good news about the blessings that America bestows on the less fortunate nations of the earth. We guarantee the freedom of the seas, send poll-watchers to apprentice democracies arranging their first elections, provide the cornucopia of goods (public and private) that sets the global standard for the label "decent standard of living." Why shouldn't we do as we please? Yes, we consume 26 percent of the world's energy supply and contribute 25 percent of the poisons to the world's atmosphere. So what? We're doing the world a favor, for crying out loud; don't make *us* sorry.

On mornings when news is scarce Caesar's heirs take up the old Roman questions about administering provinces and dispensing justice—how ought we to employ our ascendancy ("unrivaled by even the greatest empires of the past") to quiet the crowd noise in the world's dingier and more dangerous streets? The program always ends before anybody comes up with a coherent idea, and as the credits roll across the pictures of the guests congratulating one another on the subtlety of their analysis, I sometimes wonder about their grasp of history and their knowledge of geography. In what time and place do they imagine themselves temporarily on leave from Virgil's Rome? How and where do they intend to recruit the troops, and what do they think would become of America's peace and prosperity if we were to replace the story of our God-given innocence with the cynical apologetics of forthright empire?

Unlike their overlords in Washington, the American people never have been infected with the virus of imperial ambition; nor have we acquired an exalted theory of the state that might allow us to govern subject peoples with a firm hand and an easy conscience. The military academy at West Point was established in 1802 as an engineering school because the army was expected to build roads and bridges rather than to fight foreign wars. The conquest of the trans-Mississippi West was accomplished not by the march of legions but by nomadic bands crossing a succession of frontiers in the loose formation of civilian settlement. The pioneers killed anything and everything that stood in the path of progress—bears and passenger pigeons as well as Indians and buffaloes—but they seldom did so as a matter of public policy.

The imperial pretensions briefly attendant upon the Spanish-American War consisted mostly of loud speeches. At the Treaty of Versailles in 1919, Woodrow Wilson gave nobody the impression that the United States wished to rule the world. The Allied victories in the Second World War presented the United States with the semblance of an empire in a world largely reduced to ruins. If in 1941 the American presence outside the Western Hemisphere consisted of only a few islands in the Pacific, by 1945 it circled the earth, and a hastily mustered regiment of American proconsuls inherited the British oil concessions in Persia and found themselves supplying arms to Greece and grain to India, posting garrisons on the Danube and the Rhine.

But even during the years of supreme triumph the nearest that most Americans could come to an imperial habit of mind was the tone of voice in which they asked the question—of French waiters and German whores—"How much does that cost in real money?" An authentically civilian nation had acceded reluctantly to military power, and, as early as 1953, President Dwight Eisenhower, a general familiar with the stupidity and waste of war, was saying that the detonation of a single artillery shell took a year's bread out of the mouth of a starving child. The statement was both admirable and accurate but not one that would have occurred to Napoleon. The imperial adventure in Vietnam was conceived and directed by Washington bureaucrats as ignorant of war as Charles Krauthammer and Condoleezza Rice, readers of Rudyard Kipling and fans of Teddy Roosevelt who thought that an empire was as easily constructed as a movie set. The appalling failure of the production put an end to the chance of drumming up popular support for American reruns of the Pax Romana.

The absence of a citizen army prepared to fight for what it believes to be the glory of both its public and its private self obliges the Unites States to rely on increasingly expensive mercenaries. We prefer, in the old Roman phrase, "the shadow to the sun"—i.e., the luxury of sitting under silk canopies on the shaded side of the Colosseum to applaud the entertainment on the bright and sometimes painted sand. We sponsor poorer but more ferocious allies to fight proxy wars in Africa and the Middle East as well as in Asia and the Balkans, and the champions of democracy, we buy at the depressed prices paid for child labor in Chinese textile mills and Mexican strawberry fields.

America hasn't fought a war in nearly thirty years, not since our chastened helicopters lifted off the roof of the embassy in Saigon in April 1975, and I don't know why anybody would think we possess either a liking or a talent for the enterprise.[4] It's true that we maintain an army of our own—none better dressed or more expensively equipped—but it is an army made for show, a Potemkin village of an army meant to astonish Belgian bankers and frighten Arab terrorists. Our military forces are in the communications business; they send messages, they don't wage wars. The staff officers at the Pentagon know how to stage fireworks displays over Belgrade and Baghdad, how to simulate combat (aerial, naval, and ground) on state-of-the-art computer screens, where to parade the tanks on national holidays, how to deploy aircraft carriers as visual aids in the sales promotions for "the world's only superpower." All essential projects, of course, and undoubtedly worth the expenditure of $310 billion a year, but not to be con-

---

[4] I don't wish to belittle the Navy's successful sinking of a fishing boat and its quick-witted shooting down of an Iranian airliner, much less question the ability of a Marine Corps EA-6B to destroy 20 people on an Italian ski lift, but what was billed as the Persian Gulf War would have been more accurately described as a Pentagon trade show with live ammunition. Against a pitiably weak enemy—half-starved recruits, only too glad to give up their weapons for a cup of rainwater—victory was a foregone conclusion. The lack of opposition allowed us to slaughter an unknown number of Iraqis—maybe 30,000, maybe 100,000, who knows how many of them civilian—in return for 148 Americans dead in action, 35 of them killed by "friendly fire."

fused with the Normandy landings or any other expression of overt hostility in which American soldiers run the risk of being killed. The government is very clear on the point. We don't send our own troops into what the Pentagon judges to be "non-permissive environments." No sir, not in this man's army, not when a worried mother in Ohio might complain to her congressman, or when a wounded sergeant might tell a scary story to Dan Rather or Diane Sawyer.

It is the wish to remain blameless that forces up the price of the equipment. The heirs to a great military estate can afford to hire servants (some of them human, most of them electronic) to do the killing. Money in sufficient quantity washes out the stains of cruelty and greed, transports its proprietors to always higher altitudes of snow-white innocence. If the Air Force can drop bombs from 30,000 feet, preferably through a veil of fluffy white clouds, we can imagine ourselves making a war movie or playing a harmless video game. As previously noted, the work of ritual purification is best done when one knows as little as possible about who is doing what to whom. The procedure is better suited to the selling of Internet stocks and soft pornography than to the governing of empires.

August 2001

Drums Along the Potomac

New War, Old Music

As our case is new, so we must think anew, and act anew. We
must disenthrall ourselves, and then we shall save our country.
—ABRAHAM LINCOLN

The offices of *Harper's Magazine* occupy the eleventh floor
of a nineteenth-century commercial building in lower
Manhattan, east of Greenwich Village and just over a
mile north of the wreckage that was once the World Trade Center.
On the morning of September 11, I had come to work earlier than
usual, at eight instead of ten, to write my November column on
a screening of HBO's *Band of Brothers* that I'd seen the previous
Thursday evening at the Council on Foreign Relations. Produced
by Steven Spielberg and Tom Hanks as a ten-part television series,
the film was being billed as the season's newest and most exciting
portrait of America the Invincible. Against the grain of the re-
views ("shatteringly emotional," "awe-inspiring," "never to be forgotten"), I'd seen the film not as drama but as agitprop, and I

was trying to discover my reasons for the opinion when I was surprised by the sound of what I guessed to be an explosion. A distant but heavy sound, not one that I could place or remember having heard before; not a car bomb, probably not a subway tunnel. Maybe a factory in Brooklyn.

No further developments making themselves immediately audible, I returned to my recollection of the scene at the Council's handsome town house on Park Avenue and Sixty-eighth Street and to the presence of the historian Stephen Ambrose seated center stage during the discussion period, his tie sporting the pattern of the American flag, retelling the heroic tale of the D-Day landings on the beaches of Normandy in June of 1944. My notes indicated that a young woman in the after-dinner audience, an Army captain on the faculty at West Point, had asked Ambrose to speak to the secret of leadership, but before I could find the scrap of paper on which I had written down the answer (something about ancient Greeks on the plains of Troy), it occurred to me that I was listening to sirens—ambulances and fire trucks, many of them close by, none of them on the way to Brooklyn. I also noticed that although it was nearly ten o'clock, nobody else was in the office. The only television set on the premises wasn't receiving signals from the major networks, and not until I'd learned to look through the haze of static on one of the cable channels did I discover the pictures of the World Trade Center's twin towers, both of them burning.

Soon afterward other editors began to arrive in the office, their faces empty of expression, their voices dull and thin. They spoke of having seen the second explosion from a subway train on the

Manhattan Bridge, of the black shroud of smoke sprawling across the bright blue September sky, of a strange scent in the air, of bewildered crowds walking aimlessly north on Broadway. Somebody managed to bring the television broadcasts into clearer focus, and over the course of the next half hour, unable to look or turn away, saying nothing that wasn't trite ("surreal," "like a movie"), we watched the towers crumble and fall. For the rest of Tuesday we followed the news bulletins and tried to make sense of the story line. The networks played and replayed the montage of horrific images, soon familiar but always seen as if for the first time, never losing the force of a sudden and sickening blow, and I don't expect that I'll ever be rid of the sight of the United Airlines Flight 175 out of Boston coming straight at the south tower, or that of men and women, seemingly no bigger than dolls, dropping away from the windows of the north tower's upper floors, or the whirlwind of gray smoke, coiled and malevolent, devouring the light in Vesey Street.

Through the whole of Tuesday afternoon and evening the nation's leaders came before the television cameras burdened with rage and grief but at a loss to say much else except that what had happened was "unbelievable" and that the world never again would be the same. By nightfall President George W. Bush had returned from Florida to Washington, his arrival delayed by nervous hesitations at Air Force bases in Louisiana and Nebraska, and at 8:30 P.M., twelve hours after the first explosion, he addressed the American people with a not very convincing show of resolve:

"These acts of mass murder," he said, "were intended to frighten our nation into chaos and retreat. But they have failed. Our country is strong."

The message was somewhat at odds with the facts. The losses had been immense, far more terrible than anybody could have foreseen and well beyond anybody's capacity to measure or count. The country might be strong but it was badly frightened, and the chaos was unmistakable—roughly 3,000 dead in Manhattan, another 200 dead in the shambles at the Pentagon, all airline travel suspended, the White House secretaries running for their lives, a frantic sealing off of the country's nuclear power stations as well as Mount Rushmore, Disneyland, and the Liberty Bell, the New York Stock Exchange out of commission and the city's primary mayoral election postponed, telephone communications down across large sectors of the Northeast, Major League Baseball games canceled, the Capitol evacuated and most government offices in Washington closed until further notice, the military services placed on high alert.

If the President's rhetoric didn't quite meet the circumstances, neither did it account for the energy transfers—negative as well as positive—made possible by the several technological revolutions of the last thirty years, and as I listened to him speak I couldn't escape the feeling that he was reading a script not unlike the one that carried Spielberg's "band of brothers" to victory in Germany in the spring of 1945.

Wednesday's newspapers confirmed the impression. I didn't read all the reports or listen to all the television commentaries, but most of the ones that I did see and hear presented the catastrophe in the context of World War II—mobilizing the infantry and maneuvering the aircraft carriers, drawing the comparison to Pearl Harbor and declaring another day of infamy, calling out the dogs of war:

Robert Kagan, in the *Washington Post:* "Congress, in fact, should immediately declare war. It does not have to name a country."

Steve Dunleavy in the *New York Post:* "The response to this unimaginable 21st century Pearl Harbor should be as simple as it is swift—kill the bastards. . . . Train assassins. . . . Hire mercenaries. . . . As for cities or countries that host these worms, bomb them into basketball courts."

Richard Brookhiser in *The New York Observer:* "The response to such a stroke cannot be legal or diplomatic—the international equivalent of mediation, or Judge Judy. This is what we have a military for. Let's not build any more atomic bombs until we use the ones we have."

As the week passed and the full extent of the damage became increasingly apparent, the widening salients of fear (of a third or fourth attack, possibly with a nuclear or biological weapon) amplified the tone of defiance. Thousands of American flags appeared in the streets, also in store windows and flying from the fenders of cars; the television networks hardened the tag lines promoting their news programs ("America Under Attack" changed to "America's New War" and "America Rising"), and the anchorpeople abandoned the poses of objective impartiality that might be construed as unpatriotic. The Army called up the reserves; Air Force fighter planes patrolled the skies over New York and Washington; a choir of congressional voices gathered on the steps of the Capitol to bear witness to our sorrow and sing "God Bless America." President Bush declared the country at war against terrorism, not only against the individuals responsible for Tuesday's attacks but also against any country that provided them with encouragement and a headquarters tent. Between Wednesday and Saturday he made brief but firm appearances on various home fronts (with Billy Graham at the National Cathedral in Washington, among firemen and rescue workers in lower Manhattan, with his senior advisers at Camp David), and gradually he escalated the rhetorical terms of engagement—from "The First War of the Twenty-first Century" to "A New War" to the "Monumental Struggle of Good Versus Evil."[1]

Every now and then I came across somebody on television or in the newspapers saying that bold military action was not likely to put a stop to terrorism—that it was, in fact, bound to make matters worse—but the voices arguing for restraint were for the most part shouted down by the partisans of the old World War II script. Speaking for what by Sunday had become the majority

[1]On Friday, September 14, Congress granted the President the right to "use all necessary and appropriate force against those nations, organizations, or persons he determines planned, authorized, committed, or aided the terrorist attacks." Passed unanimously by the Senate, the resolution was opposed in the House of Representatives by one dissenting vote, from Barbara J. Lee (D., California), who said that military action could not guarantee the safety of the country and that "as we act, let us not become the evil we deplore."

opinion, Kagan on Wednesday in the *Washington Post* had urged the country to respond to "an attack far more awful than Pearl Harbor" with "the same moral clarity and courage" brought into the field by the "Greatest Generation." The fatuousness of his sentiment—"There's no need for nostalgia now. . . . The question is whether this generation of Americans is made of the same stuff"—clarified the reasons for my objection to *Band of Brothers* and for my disgust with the attitudes of smug self-congratulation that the screening of the film had evoked from the audience at the Council on Foreign Relations.

Everybody had been so pleased with themselves, nearly 200 guests notable for their wealth and corporate rank (presidents of banks and insurance companies, managers of media syndicates, high-ranking military officers, partners of Wall Street law firms, senior journalists) come to reaffirm their belief in the doctrine of American exceptionalism, and the whole of the evening's program had buttressed the mood of smiling self-congratulation. First a sequence of scenes from the movie, which follows the advance of a single company of the 101st Airborne Division on their perilous journey from the landing in Normandy to the crossing of the Rhine. The soft cinematography and lack of a plot reduces the effect to that of an advertisement or a recruiting poster, the soldiers in Easy Company indistinguishable not only from each other but also from a troop of young men outfitted with military accessories in a Ralph Lauren catalogue. During the after-dinner discussion, the tone of the questions suggested the flattering murmur of department-store buyers interested in the marketing strategy for an upscale men's cologne.

Several guests had heard rumors about the current generation
of recruits succumbing to the temptations of cynicism and drugs,
and Ambrose was at pains to assure them that the American Army
had recovered from its wounds in Vietnam (no more whining
complaint from Bob Dylan's harmonica), up to the task of defending Greenwich, Connecticut, and the Chase Manhattan Bank,
glad to pay the price of glory. As the author of the best-selling
book on which the film was based, Ambrose said that he'd been
touring it around the country on a literary lecture circuit and that
he often was asked whether the kids born after 1980 were capable
of "doing another D-Day."

"My answer is you're damn right they could," Ambrose said.
"They're the children of democracy. . . . American kids are
brought up to know the difference between right and wrong."

Although everybody was heartened by the news, nobody was surprised. How could it be otherwise? America had saved Western civilization in 1945, defeated Hitler and the monstrous Japanese,
conceived the Marshall Plan, distributed the gifts of trade, industry,
and lofty sentiment to the lesser nations of the earth. A supremacy
wonderful to behold, and it was good to know (while making one's
way out to the limousines standing at attention on East Sixty-
eighth Street) not only that America was beyond reproach but also
that one could live so comfortably (now and forever, world without
end) on the trust fund of liberty established on Omaha Beach and
Guadalcanal. The Greatest Generation deserved a vote of thanks.
Not only from their direct descendants but also from all the people
everywhere in the world who wished they were just like us, embracing the same values, shopping for the same prizes, endorsing the

same definitions of the good and happy life. Fortunately for the peace and safety of mankind, our triumph was complete; we were the world's only superpower and therefore (once again, a nod of thanks to the Greatest Generation) invulnerable.

My memory of the evening in the sky-booth seats of the American establishment undoubtedly has been darkened by the irony of its counterpoint to the devastation, five days later, of the Trade Center and the Pentagon, but I don't think I misrepresent the character of its easy arrogance and witless boast. I do know that I was frightened by the exhibition of what the ancient Greeks (the ones whom Ambrose left on the plains of Troy) would have recognized as the dangerous form of pride they defined as hubris. Here were people well placed within the hierarchies of American business and government, captivated by the iconography of the Pax Americana but incapable of imagining, or unwilling to acknowledge, a world other than the one they had inherited from John Wayne and Ronald Reagan and Steven Spielberg, a world in which America was not only inevitably victorious but also universally loved, its motives always pure, its principles always just, and its soldiers always welcomed by pretty French girls bearing flowers. The complacence of the American ruling class was nothing new under the sun and by no means an unfamiliar sight, but seldom had I seen it so sleek and fat, and I remember that I was anxious to get quickly away from a would-be statesman in the brokerage business telling me that we had been lucky, really privileged, to see so grand a television show.

*   *   *

Cherished illusions don't die as easily as Israeli or Palestinian children torn to pieces by a truck bomb, and in the aftermath of even so spectacular a calamity as the one visited upon New York and Washington on the morning of September 11, the majority of the television voices continued to say that what they had seen was "unbelievable." But why unbelievable? Do the merchants of the global economy not read their own sales promotions? For the last ten years the apostles of technological change have been telling the customers about the ways in which the new systems of communication confer the godlike powers of government and the freedom of nation-states upon solitary individuals seated in front of a computer in San Jose. The commercial imagery depicts a Mongolian yak herder talking on a cell phone to a fisherman in Tahiti; the ad copy reads, "We're all inter-connected," or, "Invent your own world." Do we suppose that the message doesn't translate into Urdu, that only graduates of Harvard understand the wonders of globalization (among them techniques of money-laundering and electronic encryption), or that the uses of the Internet remain beyond the grasp of Arab street people last seen as background noise in *The English Patient*?

Whoever organized the attack on the United States clearly understood not only the arcana of postmodern finance capitalism but also the idiom of the American news and entertainment media. The pictures of the World Trade Center collapsing in ruins ("shatteringly emotional," "awe-inspiring," "never to be forgotten") were made to the model of a Hollywood disaster film; not a senseless act but cost-efficient and highly leveraged, the arrival of the second plane timed to the expectation of the arriving cameras, the production values akin to those of *Independence Day* and *Air Force One* rather than *Band of Brothers*.

Why then "unbelievable," and from whom do we suppose the terrorists learned to appreciate the value of high explosives as a vivid form of speech if not from our own experiments with the genre in Iraq, Serbia, and Vietnam? Robert McNamara, the American secretary of defense in the summer of 1965, explicitly defined the bombing raids that eventually murdered upwards of two million civilians north of Saigon as a means of communication. Bombs were metaphors meant to win the North Vietnamese to a recognition of America's inevitable victory (also to an appreciation of its goodness and freedom-loving purpose), and American planes dropped what came to be known to the staff officers in the Pentagon as "bomb-o-grams." The NATO alliance adopted a similar approach to the bombardment of Belgrade in March of 1999; the targets, both military and civilian, were chosen for rhetorical rather than tactical reasons, the destruction intended to persuade Slobodan Milosevic to please read the notes being sent to him in the overly polite language of diplomacy. Again in Iraq, in 1991, we imposed harsh economic sanctions on the country in order to send a stern message to Saddam Hussein, and when Madeleine Albright, then the American secretary of state, was asked in an interview on *60 Minutes* whether she had considered the resulting death of 500,000 Iraqi children (of malnutrition and disease), she said, "We think the price is worth it."

I don't wish to argue the rights and wrongs of American foreign policy, but how do we find it incredible that other people might not have noticed the planes in the sky or the corpses in the street?

No fewer than 62 million civilians died in the the twentieth century's wars (as opposed to 43 million military personnel), buried
in mud or sand or broken stones in all seasons and every quarter
of the globe—in London and Paris as well as in Sarajevo and
Baghdad. Why not New York and Washington?

Nor have we been inattentive to the problem of motive. By
choosing to support oppressive governments in the Middle East
(in Saudi Arabia and Israel as well as in the United Arab Emirates,
and, when it suited our purposes, in Iraq), we give people reason
to think of America not as the land of the free and the home of
the brave—a democratic republic to which they might attach their
own hopes of political freedom and economic growth—but as a
corpulent empire content to place the administration of its justice
in the hands of brutal surrogates. The perception might be wrong-
headed and perverse, failing to account for the prompt deliveries
of McDonald's cheeseburgers and Arnold Schwarzenegger movies,
but the mistake is an easy one to make in Jiddah when having
one's right hand cut off for the crime of petty theft or being
sentenced to a punishment of 400 lashes for failing to heed a call
to prayer.

Almost as soon as the Trade Towers fell down, a loud caucus of
commentators and politicians began to complain about the criminal incompetence of our intelligence agencies. We should have
known. Where was the CIA? Why no timely warning or preemptive arrest? Who had neglected to alert James Bond or Bruce
Willis?

The questions missed the point. We had suffered not from a lack of data but from a failure of imagination. Accustomed to the unilateral privilege of writing the world's blockbuster geopolitical scripts, hiring the cast and paying for the special effects, the Washington studio executives seldom take the trouble to look at the movie from the point of view of an audience that might be having trouble with the subtitles. Why bother? Let them eat pop-corn and look at the pictures. It isn't only that we don't learn the language.[2] We don't remember history. Obliged to issue a state-ment to the cameras while traveling to Washington on September 11, President Bush began by saying, "Freedom itself was attacked this morning by a faceless coward." Two days later he was talking about mindless hatred and unfathomable evil.

But it wasn't freedom that had been attacked; an abstract rather than a proper noun, freedom is as safe as love or justice from the effects of burning kerosene and collapsing steel. Nor were the attackers faceless or their hatred mindless. The networks were proud to show their photo album of Osama bin Laden (romantic bandit once associated with the CIA), and it wasn't difficult to find university professors prepared to discuss the reasons why at least some of the Arabs in the Middle East might have nurtured a long and bitter grievance against the American presence in Israel and the Persian Gulf.

---

[2]Five days after the September 11 attack Mike Wallace interviewed two senior officials formerly charged with directing the CIA's intelligence operations in the Middle East and Afghanistan. Neither of them spoke fluent Arabic. Similarly, during the entire twelve years of the Vietnam War, only one American university offered graduate instruction in the Vietnamese language.

The history lesson was too hard to set to the music of trumpets
and drums, and most of the media voices (politicians, generals,
anchorpersons) chose to place the attack in the self-referential context of the great American shopping mall. Obviously the terrorists
wanted everything in all the suburban show windows, wanted to
drive a Lexus, own a beach house in East Hampton, wear an Ar-
mani suit. Unhappily, they couldn't afford the prices because, in
the phrase of one of the experts on CBS, "They hadn't done too
well in the modern world." Thus their envy and resentment. An
expression of childish rage or a proof of possession by the Devil.
Nothing to do with history or politics, let alone a philosophical
objection or a legitimate argument against a global economic order, largely denominated in American money, that decides what
other people shall produce, what they will be paid for their labor,
how they live, and when they die. Reading the few commentators
attempting to parse the theory of Islamic jihad, I was reminded
of the anarchist movement in late-nineteenth-century Europe, and
of Barbara Tuchman's chapter on the topic in *The Proud Tower,* an
aptly titled book about another age of wealth and ease rudely
awakened from its dream of moral sovereignty. Utopian in their
thinking and certainly not crazy, the anarchist prophets, among
them Michael Bakunin, Pierre Proudhon, and Prince Peter Kro-
potkin, defined all government (under any name, in any form) as
a synonym for slavery, the laws (in any form, under any name)
"cobwebs for the rich and chains of steel for the poor."[3] They

3Proudhon's excoriation of government prefigures the proclamations of the Islamic jihad as well as those of Timothy McVeigh and the Unabomber—"To be

sought to destroy the systems in place (the secular consumer society then known, more simply, as the bourgeoisie) with what they called "the propaganda of the deed." The assassins, usually Latins or Slavs, threw their bombs at kings and opera houses (the symbolic targets of the day), and although they were invariably seized soon afterward by the army or the police, they went defiantly to death, fierce zealots (not mindless, not faceless, not cowards) carrying their passion to the scaffold or the guillotine, willing to sacrifice their lives on what they called "the altar of the Idea."[4]

The nineteenth-century enemies of the Gilded Age, like the contemporary believers in the Islamic jihad, had no political program in mind, no interest in labor reform or the redistributions of wealth. On behalf of what they thought was revealed truth, they wished to make an apocalyptic statement, to annihilate "mankind's tormentors," whom Bakunin listed as "priests, monarchs,

governed is to be watched, inspected, spied on, regulated, indoctrinated, preached at, controlled, ruled, censored, by persons who have neither wisdom nor virtue. It is every action and transaction to be registered, stamped, taxed, patented, licensed, assessed, measured, reprimanded, corrected, frustrated. Under pretext of the public good it is to be exploited, monopolized, embezzled, robbed and then, at the least protest or word of complaint, to be fined, harassed, vilified, beaten up, bludgeoned, disarmed, judged, condemned, imprisoned, shot, garroted, deported, sold, betrayed, swindled, deceived, outraged, dishonored."

[4]Six heads of state were assassinated in the name of anarchism in the twenty years prior to 1914. "They were President Carnot of France in 1894, Premier Canovas of Spain in 1897, Empress Elizabeth of Austria in 1898, King Humbert of Italy in 1900, President McKinley of the United States in 1901, and another Premier of Spain, Canalejas, in 1912.

statesmen, soldiers, officials, financiers, capitalists, moneylenders, lawyers"—a.k.a. each and every member of the Council on Foreign Relations, myself among them, no matter how blameless our individual consciences or how generous our contributions to the Public Broadcasting System.

No sum of historical justification can excuse the attack on the World Trade Center and the Pentagon, but neither can we excuse our own arrogance behind the screens of shock and disbelief. Enthralled by an old script, we didn't see the planes coming because we didn't think we had to look.

November 2001

Res Publica

There is nothing stable in the world; uproar's your only music.
                                                    —JOHN KEATS

Throughout the month of October the fire continued to
burn in the ruin of lower Manhattan, and the numerous
politicians who came to look upon the face of apocalyptic
destruction never failed to see, somewhere behind the veil of ran-
cid and still-drifting smoke, an American phoenix rising from the
ashes. None of them pretended to a close acquaintance with the
miraculous bird, but the metaphor was never far from their
thought when they spoke of a renewed sense of national unity and
purpose, of democracy regained and liberty reborn, of the American spirit, eagle-feathered and indomitable, shining with the
promise of a new day's dawn.

Given the ground on which the speakers stood (a makeshift
cemetery in which 3,000 of their fellow citizens lay buried under

1.2 million tons of fallen concrete and twisted steel), it was impossible to doubt the truth of their emotion or the honesty of
their intent. What was more difficult to judge was the portrait of
the future they had in mind. Almost as soon as they had said that
America never again would be the same, they began to talk about
the restoration of the familiar and heroic past, making good the
losses of September 11 with quicker-witted intelligence agents,
heavier artillery, more patriotic displays of consumer confidence
in all the nation's better stores. If the fine words didn't amount
to much when weighed for the content of their thought or meaning, possibly it was because the destruction of the World Trade
Center also obliterated most of the supporting theory that for the
last twenty years had buttressed the American claim to an advanced state of economic and political enlightenment. As construed by the household sophists in the Reagan Administration
and endorsed by their successors in the Bush and Clinton administrations, the intellectual foundation for the country's wealth and
happiness rested on four pillars of imperishable wisdom:

1. Big government is by inclination Marxist, by definition
   wasteful and incompetent, a conspiracy of fools indifferent to the welfare of the common man. The best government is no government. The agencies of big government
   stand as acronyms for overbearing bureaucracy, as synonyms for poverty, indolence, and disease.

2. Global capitalism is the eighth wonder of the world, a
   light unto the nations and the answer to everybody's

prayers. Nothing must interfere with its sacred mysteries and omniscient judgment.

3. The art of politics (embarrassingly human and therefore corrupt) is subordinate to the science of economics (reassuringly abstract and therefore perfect). What need of political principle or philosophy when it is the money markets that set policy, pay the troops, distribute alms? What need of statesmen, much less politicians, when it isn't really necessary to know their names or remember what they say?

4. History is at an end. The new world economic order vanquished the last of the skeptics by refuting the fallacy of Soviet Communism. Having reached the final stopping place on the road to ideological perfection, mankind no longer need trouble itself with any new political ideas. Francis Fukuyama, an author much admired by the *Wall Street Journal,* summed up the proposition in a sentence deemed sublime, "For our purposes, it matters very little what strange thoughts occur to people in Albania or Burkina Faso. . . ."

All four pillars of imperishable wisdom perished on the morning of September 11, reduced within an hour to the incoherence of the rubble in Liberty Street. By noon even the truest of true believers knew that they had been telling themselves a fairy tale. If not to big government, then where else did the friends of laissez-faire economics look for the rescue of their finances and the saving of their lives; if not the agencies of big government, who then brought the ambulances from as far away as Albany or sent the firemen into the doomed buildings with no promise of a finder's fee? It wasn't the free market that hijacked the airplanes and cross-promoted them into bombs, or Adam Smith's invisible hand that cut the throats of the pilots on what they thought was a flight to Los Angeles. History apparently was still a work in progress, the strange thoughts grown in the basements of Tirana possibly closer to the geopolitical spirit of the times than the familiar platitudes handed around the conference tables at the American Enterprise Institute.

By nightfall the revelation was complete, and during the weeks since September 11 the rush into the shelters of big government has come to resemble the crowding of sinners into the tent of a prairie evangelist. The corporate lobbyists make daily pilgrimages to Washington in search of federal subsidy; the Air Force bombs Afghanistan; the White House and the State Department revise the terms of our diplomacy with Russia, Pakistan, Saudi Arabia, Israel, and China; the FBI sets up our defenses against the airborne spores of anthrax, and the once-gaudy advertisements for what was variously billed as the globalist hegemony and the new world economic order begin to look like faded circus posters peeling from a roadside billboard in eastern Tennessee. Every morning's paper and every evening's television broadcast punch a new hole in the old story, and it turns out that public service on behalf of the common good (as recently as last August thought no longer fashionable or pertinent) retains at least the memory of an honorable meaning. Mayor Rudolph Giuliani in New York gives voice to the city's courage, and among an electorate formerly presumed decadent the discovery of such a thing as an American commonwealth finds expression not only in the show of flags but also in the myriad voluntary acts of citizenship—unpaid rescue workers clearing the wreckage in lower Manhattan, $850 million in emergency funds contributed by individuals as well as corporations, the news media accepting substantial loss of advertising revenue in order to provide more time and space for the discovery of maybe necessary information, a generous upwelling of tolerance and compassion among people of different colors, their regard for one another grounded in the recognition that the modifying adjectives (black, gay, white, native, etc.) matter less than the noun American.

By the end of October it had been generally understood that America no longer enjoyed a special arrangement with Providence, preserved by the virtue of its inhabitants and the grace of its geography from the provocations of death, chance, kings, and desperate men. Confronted with determined enemies (many of them still unknown, some of them armed with appalling weapons) the nation stood exposed, like other nations, to the insults of outrageous fortune. The awareness of the predicament (on the part of both the politicians at the microphones and the voters in the streets) conceivably could lead to a reconstitution of the American idea, but the finding of the phoenix in the ashes presupposes a debate rising from an intellectual structure a good deal sturdier than the one lost in the wreckage of the World Trade Center. I imagine the argument falling along the division between the people who would continue the American experiment and those who think that the experiment has gone far enough, and if I can't frame all the questions that might well be asked, I can think of at least a few:

How high a price do we set on the head of freedom? If we delete another few paragraphs from the Bill of Rights (for our own protection, of course, in the interest of peace, prosperity, and carefree summer vacations), what do we ask of the state in return for our silence in court? Do we wish to remain citizens of a republic, or do we prefer the forms of participatory fascism in which the genial man on horseback assures us that repression is good for the soul? With what secular faith do we match the zeal of militant Islam and combat the enmity of the impoverished peoples of the earth to whom the choice between war and peace presents itself as a choice of no significance? How define the American democracy as a *res publica* for which we might willingly give up our lives? Our own lives, not the lives of foreign legions. And of what does the *res publica* consist?

None of the questions lead to certain answers, but if we don't ask them of ourselves I don't know how we can expect to rediscover the American idea in a world unknown to Jefferson. Assume a conversation at least as long as the war that President Bush forecasts for the mountains of Afghanistan, and we might begin by strengthening the habit of dissent and improving our powers of observation. The barbarism in Washington doesn't dress itself in the costumes of the Taliban; it wears instead the smooth-shaven smile of a Senate resolution sold to the highest bidder—for the drilling of the Arctic oil fields or the lifting from the rich the burden of the capital-gains tax, for bigger defense budgets, reduced medical insurance, enhanced surveillance, grotesque monopoly. If we took more of an interest in the making of our foreign policy, usually for the profit of our corporate overlords rather than for the safety of the American people, maybe we would know why, when bringing the lamp of liberty to the darker places of the earth, the United States invariably chooses for its allies the despots who operate their countries on the model of a prison or a jail. We might even wonder why, ten years ago during the denouement of the Gulf War, George Bush the elder chose to leave an army in Saudi Arabia. Did we mean to protect our supply of cheap oil, or were we providing the Saudi ruling family with household troops to preserve them from a revolutionary uprising led by malcontents as clever as Osama bin Laden?

If we mean to project abroad the force of the *res publica* made glorious by the death of American teenagers and Muslim holy men, we might want to consider taking better care of our own domestic commonwealth. For the last twenty years we've let fall into disrepair nearly all of the public infrastructure—roads, water systems, schools, power plants, bridges, hospitals, broadcast frequencies—that provides the country with a foundation for its common enterprise. The privatization of the nation's public resources has enriched the investors fortunate enough to profit from the changes of venue, but at what cost to our sense of general well-being? The lopsided division of the country into the factions of the hapless many and the privileged few has allowed our faith in the republic to degenerate from the strength of a conviction into the weakness of a sentiment. By discounting what the brokers classify as "non-market values," we're left with a body politic defined not as the union of its collective energies and hopes but as an aggregate of loosely affiliated selfish interests (ethnic, regional, commercial, sexual), armed with their own manifestos, loyal to their own agendas, secure in the compounds of their own languages. Democracy understood as a fancy Greek name for the American Express card and the Neiman Marcus Christmas catalogue, the government seen as a Florida resort hotel, its assortment of goods and services deserving of respect in the exact degree to which it satisfies the whims of its patrons and meets the expectations of comfort and style at both the discount and holiday rates.

As was proved by events on the morning of September 11, the laissez-faire theories of government do us an injustice. They don't speak to the best of our character; neither do they express the cherished ideal embodied in the history of a courageous people. What joins the Americans one to another is not a common nationality, race, or ancestry but their voluntary pledge to a shared work of both the moral and political imagination. My love of country follows from my love of its freedoms, not from pride in its armies or its fleets, and I admire the institutions of American government as useful and well-made tools (on the order of a plow, an axe, or a surveyor's plumb line) meant to support the liberties of the people, not the ambitions of the state. The Constitution serves as the premise for a narrative rather than as the design for a monument or a plan for an invasion.

Any argument about the direction of the American future becomes an argument between the past and present tense. Let us hope that it proves to be both angry and fierce. The friends of the status quo (both houses of Congress, most of the national news media, the Hollywood patriots, and a legion of corporate spokespersons) already have made it clear that they prefer as little discussion as possible. Domestic political dissent they regard as immoral and, in time of war, treasonous. They believe it their duty to invest President Bush not only with the powers of a monarch but also with the attribute of wisdom. Put out more flags, post more guards, distribute the pillows of cant. Maybe two or three years from now, when all the terrorists have been rounded up and the Trade Center towers replaced with a golden statue of Mammon, the time will come to talk of politics. In the meanwhile, my children, while waiting for that far-off happy day, follow directions, submit to the surveillance, look at the nice pictures brought to you by the Pentagon, know that your rulers are wise.

So sayeth Trent Lott and *Time* magazine, and the admonition seems to me as feckless as the theory that supported last summer's pillars of imperishable wisdom. The country at the moment stands in need of as many questions as anybody can think to ask. Rightly understood, democracy is an uproar—nothing quiet, orderly, or safe—and among all the American political virtues, candor is probably the one most necessary to the success of our shared enterprise; unless we try to tell one another the truth about what we know and think and see, we might as well amuse ourselves (for as long as somebody else allows us to do so) with Steven Spielberg movies.

Alfred North Whitehead once observed that it is the business of the future to be dangerous (not because the future is perverse but because it doesn't know how to be anything else), and whether we like it or not, the argument now in progress in Moscow and Jerusalem and Islamabad is the same argument that enlivened the annals of republican Rome, built the scaffolds of the Spanish Inquisition, and gave rise to the American Revolution. If we fail to engage it, we do so at our peril. The freedoms of expression present democratic societies with the unwelcome news that they are in trouble, but because all societies, like most individuals, are always in some kind of trouble, the news doesn't drive them onto the reefs of destruction. They die instead from the fear of thought and the paralysis that accompanies the wish to believe that only the wicked perish.

December 2001

American Jihad

War is the health of the state.
—RANDOLPH BOURNE

Fascism should more properly be called corporatism, since it is
the merger of state and corporate power.
—BENITO MUSSOLINI

*T*hree months ago I thought we'd been given a chance for
a conversation about the future of the American political
idea, the attacks on the Pentagon and the World Trade
Center providing an impressive occasion for timely remarks on the
topics of our foreign and domestic policy as well as an opportunity
to ask what we mean by the phrases "public service," "common
good," "civic interest." The newspapers were reporting daily proofs
of selfless citizenship, not only on the part of the volunteers clearing the wreckage in lower Manhattan but also on the part of
people everywhere else in the country giving of their money and
effort to whatever need was nearest at hand, and I expected some-

thing of the same public-spiritedness to find a voice in the Congress, in the major news media, possibly on the television talk shows. Informed argument about why and how America had come to be perceived as a dissolute empire; instructive doubts cast on the supposed omniscience of the global capital markets; sustained questioning of the way in which we divide the country's wealth; a distinction drawn between the ambitions of the American national security state and the collective well-being of the American citizenry.

By December I knew that I'd been barking at the moon. The conversation maybe had a chance of taking place in magazines of small circulation, or possibly somewhere in the distant reaches of C-SPAN (at two A.M., on the stage of a college auditorium in Wabash, Indiana), but not in the chambers of Congress, not under the circus tents of the big-time news and entertainment media, not, except by special permission and then only with a word of apology, on network television.

Ted Koppel struck the preferred note of caution on November 2 when introducing his *Nightline* audience to Arundhati Roy, an Indian novelist and a critic of the American bombing of Afghanistan:

"Some of you, many of you, are not going to like what you hear tonight. You don't have to listen. But if you do, you should know that dissent sometimes comes in strange packages. . . ."

Most of the other security guards deciding what could and could not be seen on camera explained the absence of talking heads critical of the American "War on Terrorism" by saying that they couldn't find any credible experts inclined to make an argument both seditious and absurd. Thus Erik Sorenson, president of MSNBC, telling a reporter from the *New York Times* that apart from the raving of a few Hollywood celebrities there wasn't enough dissent in the country "to warrant coverage." Or Peter Beinart, editor of *The New Republic,* outraged by the noise of protest in the streets:

"This nation is now at war. And in such an environment, domestic political dissent is immoral without a prior statement of national solidarity, a choosing of sides."

In other words, as President Bush had become fond of saying to United Nations ambassadors and foreign heads of state, "Either you are with us, or you're with the terrorists."

As a means of quieting the distemper of the press, nothing works as well as the anodyne of war. Caught up in the memory of a tale told by Homer or Rudyard Kipling, the keepers of the nation's conscience gladly smother the peepings of dissent and quickly learn to stuff a sock into the mouth of an impiety. Show them a cruise missile or a map, and they become more ferocious than the generals. The scouts for the Sunday talk shows might have found it difficult to recruit skeptics, but they didn't have any trouble enlisting fuglemen to blow the trumpets of imperial advance—Tom Brokaw, impatiently wanting to know why the Army wasn't deploying ground troops, "in division-size force" somewhere south of Kabul; Dick Morris on Fox News, urging the Pentagon to boldly extend Civilization's War Against Barbarism by occupying Libya and invading Iraq.

The eagerness to enlarge the theater of military operations—a strategy endorsed not only by the regimental commanders at

Fox News but also by Newt Gingrich, Henry Kissinger, and Senator John McCain—seemed as senseless as the elevation of Osama bin Laden to a world figure on the scale of Fidel Castro or Charles de Gaulle, but by the end of October I'd begun to understand that the heavily armored media commentary fortified a broadcast studio and went well with flags, the rhetoric made of the same red, white, and blue bunting that decorates the speeches of President Bush—"We go forward to defend freedom and all that is good and just in the world," "We value the right to speak our minds," "Our ultimate victory is assured." The viewing audience isn't expected to know what the words mean; we're supposed to listen to them in the way one listens to a military band playing "Stars and Stripes Forever" on the Washington Mall, or to Ray Charles singing "God Bless America" in a World Series baseball park.

Language degraded into the currency of propaganda doesn't lend itself to conversations about the future course of the American political idea, and if in September I thought that the destruction of the World Trade Center and the Pentagon might teach us something about our own history as well as furnishing us with an English translation of the Arabic word for "student," it was because I'd neglected to ask where the profit was to be found in a cloud of black smoke rising from the ruin of lower Manhattan. Where was the silver lining, and where the blessings in disguise? *Qui bono?*, the oldest of the old maxims once learned in a high school Latin class. To what end, and in whose interest, do we astonish the world with the magnificence of "Operation Enduring Freedom"?

The attacks on the buildings in Virginia and New York were abominable and unprovoked, inflicting an as yet unspecified sum of damage and an as yet incalculable measure of grief, but, as Sir Michael Howard recently remarked to a lecture audience in London, they didn't constitute an act of war. By choosing to define them as such, we invested a gang of murderous criminals with the sovereignty of a nation-state (or, better yet, with the authority of a world-encircling religion) and declared war on both an unknown enemy and an abstract noun. Like an Arab jihad against capitalism, the American jihad against terrorism cannot be won or lost; nor does it ever end. We might as well be sending the 101st Airborne Division to conquer lust, annihilate greed, capture the sin of pride. Howard regards the careless use of language as "a very natural but terrible and irrevocable error." If so, it is an error that works to the advantage of the American political, military, and industrial interests that prefer the oligarchic and corporatist forms of government to those of a democracy.

Absent the excitements of a foreign war, in what domestic political accident might we not have lost the wooden figurehead of President George Bush? Six months ago we were looking at a man so obviously in the service of the plutocracy that he could have been mistaken for a lawn jockey in the parking lot of a Houston golf club or a prize fish mounted on the wall of a Jacksonville bank. Having signed the law awarding $1.4 trillion of tax relief to the country's richest individuals, he'd reimbursed the people who had paid his ticket to the White House, but the smiling pose of "compassionate conservatism" was becoming hard to hold amidst the gradual recognition of both its fraudulence and its rigidity. The economy was in trouble, the Senate had lost its Republican majority, the President's approval ratings were sliding into recession, and too many people still were wondering about the sleights-of-hand that won the electoral vote in Florida. All in all, not a promising outlook for a politician who had been told, and so believed, that the running of a government was no different than the management of a corporation.

On September 11, like Pinocchio brushed with the good fairy's wand on old Gepetto's shelf of toys, the wooden figurehead turned into flesh and blood. A great leader had been born, within a month compared (by David Broder in the *Washington Post*) to Abraham Lincoln. Suddenly we were looking at a man resplendent on the gilded throne of power, his clichéd speeches revealed as "Churchillian" in the bright new morning of a war that Secretary of Defense Donald Rumsfeld guessed might last as long as forty years.

Which was, of course, good news for the defense industries and the military establishment. The Senate wasn't slow to take the point, voting, unanimously and without debate on October 2, to fund a $60 billion missile-defense system that to the best of nearly everybody's knowledge can't hit its celestial targets and offers no defense against the deadly weapons (smallpox virus, dynamite stuffed into a barrel of nuclear waste, etc.) likely to be delivered in rented trucks. But why bother with cowardly and disloyal argument? The nation is at war; civilization trembles in the balance, and what true American stoops to haggle over the price of freedom?

If the Senate cannot bring itself to question a proposition as false as the missile-defense system, then what may we not expect in the months of crisis yet to come? The Navy will want bigger aircraft carriers, the Air Force another four hundred planes, the Army a set of tanks equipped with electronics so sophisticated that they can set up the targeting coordinates for each of the Koran's ninety-nine names for God.

Senator Carl Levin (D., Mich.), chairman of the Armed Services Committee, attributed the lack of debate about the missiles to the need for "unity" when America was under siege; similar flows of sentiment stifled the asking of rude questions about the war's long-term aims and short-term costs. The Democratic members in both houses of the Congress as silent as the chairs; no memorable speech or hint of eloquence; nothing but an obedient show of hands and the hushed thumping of rubber stamps.

Addressing a joint session of Congress on the evening of September 20 the President congratulated the assembled politicians for their bravery in a time of trouble, thanking them "for what you have already done, and for what we will do together." Fortunately for the friends of good government, the patriotic news media have quarantined the tone of irony for the duration of the campaign against the world's "evildoers"; otherwise the President's speech might have evoked not only a round of brisk applause but also a gust of appreciative laughter. What the Congress had been doing (in concert with the White House and the federal regulatory agencies and brazen with the pretense of assisting the war effort) was looting the country's public interest on behalf of its well-placed private interests—the Interior Department relieved of its power to veto mining projects on public lands; the pharmaceutical companies negotiating the right to sell their drugs at the customary high prices in the event of a biological or biochemical catastrophe; the insurance industry collectively seeking a $10 billion deductible; best of all, the economic "stimulus package" passed on October 24 by the House of Representatives in the amount of $101 billion, the bulk of the stimulant administered to wealthy individuals and corporations.

Asked about the apparent senselessness of the repeal of the corporate alternative minimum tax, Dick Armey (R., Tex.), the House majority leader, justified the gifts ($1.4 billion to I.B.M., $833 million to G.M., $671 million to G.E., etc.) by saying, "This country is in the middle of a war. Now is not the time to provoke spending confrontations with our Commander-in-Chief." In answer to a related question as to why the $15 billion soothing of economic wounds suffered by the airline industry didn't allot any money, none whatsoever, to the 150,000 airline workers who had lost their jobs in September, Armey observed that any help extended to such people "is not commensurate with the American spirit."

Who but a decadent Arab could have thought otherwise? Like Senator Levin, Congressman Armey understood that in time of war the United States can't afford the distraction of petty domestic politics. The promise of prescription-drug benefits for the elderly will have to wait; so will nearly everything else that most people associate with the words "national security"—repair of the nation's roads and schools and the prospect of decent health care for the 43 million citizens who can't afford to buy it at the going rate.

The country's corporate overlords don't associate the phrase "national security" with the health and well-being of the American public; they define the term as a means of acquiring wealth and as a reason for directing the country's diplomacy toward policies that return a handsome profit—the bombing of caves in the Hindu Kush preferred to the building of houses in St. Louis or Detroit. The work goes more smoothly when conducted in an atmosphere of constant dread, and how better to magnify that dread than by declaring a war against terrorism? Enemies on every hand and all of them unseen; nothing safe, not even a postcard from a maiden aunt. Happy to be of service and proud to protect the American people not only from bearded strangers but also from themselves, the Congress in September hurried to the task of forging legal shackles and restraints, also to the broadening of the government's police powers and the further destruction of the Bill of Rights. By the end of October the President had signed the USA PATRIOT Act, 342 pages of small print that hardly anybody in the Senate or the House of Representatives took the trouble to read but which nevertheless permitted the attorney general to expand telephone and Internet surveillance, extend the reach of wiretaps, open financial and medical records to searches for suspicious behavior and criminal intent. Two weeks later he signed an emergency order (conceding that it set aside "the principles of law and the rules of evidence") allowing him to remand to a military tribunal any foreign national about whom he had "reason to believe" a rumor of cohabitation with a terrorist organization, a nihilist author, or an anarchist idea. The F.B.I. in the meantime was rounding up legal immigrants of Middle Eastern descent (5,000 of them as of November 15) to inquire about their connections to Saladin and the Third Crusade. Although the corporatist distaste for the Constitution is nothing new (cf., the deliberate weakening of the First, Fourth, and Sixth Amendments over the last twenty years), the guarantee of an always present danger extends the government's prerogative to enforce whatever rule of law happens to prove convenient to the rule of money.

On November 11 in Atlanta, standing in front of a photomontage of heroic New York City firemen, President Bush told his audience that the nation "faces a threat to our freedoms, and the stakes could not be higher." What he said was true, but not in the way that he intended. We have more to fear from the fatwas issued in Washington than from those drifting across the deserts of Central Asia. The agents of Al Qaeda might wreck our buildings and disrupt our commerce, maybe even manage to kill a number of our fellow citizens, but we do ourselves far greater harm if we pawn our civil rights and consign the safekeeping of our liberties to Mullah John Ashcroft and the mujahedeen in the hospitality tents of American crusade.

January 2002

Mythography

> Our world has sprouted a weird concept of security and a
> warped sense of morality. Weapons are sheltered like treasures
> and children are exposed to incineration.
> —BERTRAND RUSSELL

For the last four months the curators of the national news media have done their patriotic best to muffle objections to our worldwide crusade against terrorism, the editors of important newspapers removing contraband opinion from the manuscripts of known polemicists, the producers of network talk shows softening the criticisms of American foreign policy for fear that they otherwise might be seen as displays of weak-mindedness if not as proofs of treason. I don't wonder why the watchers at the gate of freedom might want to keep a sharp lookout for suspicious substances at a time when some of them had received anthrax in the mail, but I didn't think that we were well on the way to a ministry of state propaganda until I came across

"Defending Civilization," a guide to the preferred forms of free speech issued last November in Washington by the American Council of Trustees and Alumni.

Knowing little else about the organization except what could be inferred from the writings of the conservative and neoconservative ideologues prominently identified as its leading lights (among them Lynne V. Cheney, the vice president's wife and a fellow of the American Enterprise Institute; Martin Peretz, chairman of *The New Republic;* Irving Kristol, co-editor of *The Public Interest;* and William Bennett, editor of *The Book of Virtues*), I took it as a given that the document would read like a sermon preached against the wickedness of the 1960s and the great darkness brought down upon the nation's universities by the werewolves of the intellectual left. It's an old sermon, discredited by the facts but still much beloved by the parties of the right, and I was prepared for the ritual scourgings of Eros, multiculturalism, and modernity. I expected cant; I didn't expect the bringing of what amounted to a charge of sedition against any university or scholar therein failing to pledge allegiance to the sovereign wisdom of President George W. Bush. I've had occasion to read a good deal of fourth-rate agitprop over the last thirty years, but I don't remember an argument as disgraceful as the one advanced by the American Council of Trustees and Alumni under the rubric of "academic freedom, quality and accountability"; if to no other purpose than that of appreciating its unctuousness and dishonesty, I think it worth the trouble of a brief review.

Proceeding from the assumption that the nation's universities—
all the nation's universities—wander in a desert of ignorance,
the report sets out to show that the nation's universities—all
the nation's universities—failed to respond to the provocation of
September 11 with a proper degree of "anger, patriotism, and
support of military intervention." Right-thinking people everywhere else in the country were quick to recognize evil when
they saw it, prompt in their exhibition of American flags,
wholehearted in their rallying to the cause of virtue. "Not so in
academe." Most university professors succumbed to "moral rela-
tivism"; "Some even pointed accusatory fingers," not at the terrorists but at their fellow Americans. So monstrous was the
betrayal that "the message of much of academe was clear:
BLAME AMERICA FIRST."

Although careful to make its curtsy to "the robust exchange of
ideas" so "essential to a free society," the report makes little effort
to conceal the stench of its intolerance. America's universities had
proved themselves "distinctly equivocal" in their response to the
nation's sorrow, and it was important to remember—"never more
so than in these unsettling times"—that "Academic freedom does
not mean freedom from criticism."

As evidence for its grotesque assertions, the report offers a list
of 115 subversive remarks culled from college newspapers, or over-
heard on university campuses by the Council's vigilant informants,
during the fifty-one days between September 14 and November
4. The following citations can be taken as representative of the
sentiments deemed traitorous or un-American:

" 'We have to learn to use courage for peace instead of war.'
    —Professor of Religious Studies, Pomona College

" '[I]ntolerance breeds hate, hate breeds violence and violence
breeds death, destruction and heartache.'
            —Student, University of Oklahoma

" '[We should] build bridges and relationships, not simply
bombs and walls.'
        —Speaker at Harvard Law School

" 'Our grief is not a cry for war.'
        —Poster at New York University"

I wish I thought the Council's paranoia confined to a small
company of reclusive minutemen, outfitted with hunting rifles,
and gathered around a campfire in Idaho or Montana. Unhappily,
I suspect that the report accurately reflects the attitudes widely
distributed among the upper servants of government and the news
media, consistent with the judgments of Attorney General John
Ashcroft, at one with the 90 percent approval rating accorded to
the diplomacy of President Bush.

Words pressed into the service of propaganda lose the name and
form of meaning, a point of which I was reminded when, at about
the same time I encountered the Washington tract, I happened to
read *The Psychology of War,* a study of the ways in which human
beings adjust their interpretations of reality in order to recognize
the mass murder of other human beings as glorious adventure and

noble enterprise. First published in 1992 but fortunately brought back into print this year by the Allworth Press, the book, written by Lawrence LeShan, draws a distinction between the "sensory" and the "mythic" perceptions of war. Let war become too much of a felt experience, as close at hand as the putrid smell of rotting flesh or the presence of a newly headless corpse seated in a nearby chair, and most people tend to forget to sing patriotic songs. Much better for everybody's morale if the war takes place in a galaxy far, far away, in the mountains of high-sounding abstraction where only the enemy dies.

LeShan observes that governments wishing to produce successful, award-winning wars must be sure to reserve the right to what Hollywood film directors know as the final cut. Governments that fail to do so (allowing control of the script to escape into the hands of imperfectly indoctrinated journalists) give up the chance of transposing the war into the realm of myth (there to take its heroic place with World Wars I and II), and they're apt to lose both the viewing public and the next election. The critical and commercial failure of the wars in Korea and Vietnam demonstrated the unwillingness of the American people to regard themselves as imperialists, also their distaste for wars conducted in the sensory theaters of operation.

It's never easy to stage a mythic war, particularly a war in which, by definition, the civilian population becomes the primary target, and as if to illustrate the difficulties confronted by the apostles of never-ending crusade, New Line Cinema on December 19 of last year positioned the opening of *The Lord of the Rings* to compete for the Christmas box office against the Pentagon's production of "The Fall of Kandahar," then in its second month of national and international release. Despite certain similarities (President Bush as wholesome a protagonist as Frodo Baggins, the landscape of Afghanistan as desolate as Gorgoroth and Nurn), the government documentary suffered by comparison with the Hollywood romance—the cinematography not as good and the pacing embarrassingly slow; too many pointless repetitions; the characters ineptly named (Rumsfeld and Rice instead of Aragorn, Peregrin Pippin, and Gimli, the dwarf); no elves, too few mithril-coats, not nearly enough ringwraiths or wizards.

Lacking symbols of good and evil as formidable as the Dark Lord of Mordor and Gandalf the Grey, the studio executives in Washington rely on the genies in the bottles of technology and the telling of the story in the language of a fairy tale. Fortunately for the safety of the republic, the capacity of our defense industries cannot be matched by any country in the world—not now, probably not ever before in the history of mankind. Making weapons is what we know how to do best, the supreme achievement of late-twentieth-century American civilization. To this blessed work we assign our finest intellect and the largest share of our treasure, and in the magnificence of an aircraft carrier or a cruise missile we find our moral and aesthetic equivalent of the Sistine ceiling and Chartres Cathedral.

But if the government need not worry about a shortage of special effects—the Pentagon's laser-guided bombs as stealthy in approach and as deadly in result as one of J.R.R. Tolkien's Nazgûls—the mythologizing of the plot requires the collaboration of a news media eager to bring urgent bulletins, every hour on the hour, from the frontiers of dread. The Pentagon provided the illustrations and nursery-rhyme texts, and if the dispatches from the few reporters actually on the ground in Kabul or Mazar-i-Sharif tended to present the Taliban as ragged fugitives—lightly armed, often barefoot, their cause lost without a fight—the editors in Washington and New York strengthened the adjectives, brushed out the footage of dogs devouring dead bodies on the road to Kunduz, dressed up the headlines with "monsters" and "diabolical henchmen" overseeing "a web of hate." Geraldo Rivera went off to the Khyber Pass with a pistol in his luggage, informing his viewers on FOX News that he would consider killing Osama bin Laden if the chance presented itself somewhere on the snowy heights of Tora Bora.

When temporarily at a loss for melodrama, the news media applied to government officials for grim predictions or to university professors for dire warnings. Important members of Congress could be relied upon to demand the immediate subjugation of Iraq; various historians obligingly mentioned "the clash of civilizations" and an Arab host gathered on the plain of Armageddon under the glittering banners of militant Islam. Never mind that as of the first week in December the djinns of Al Qaeda were still nowhere to be found, and that what little could be seen of their abandoned crevices and holes suggested the improbability of their resemblance either to the Variags of Khand or to Suleiman the Just.

Failing to drum up a threat from an informed congressional

or academic source, the authors of the daily allegory appealed to weapons experts and to theorists fluent in the jargon of Cold War realpolitik. Several such authorities took part in a round-table discussion published as a special Thanksgiving issue of *The National Interest,* a journal that lists Henry Kissinger as cochairman of its editorial board, and on reading the transcript I remember thinking that the dialogue sounded like the muttering of orcs in the last chapters of *The Lord of the Rings*. Somebody said that the time had come to "flip" Iran (presumably from a low-growth theocracy to a high-yield democracy), and Dimitri Simes, president of The Nixon Center, said no, this wasn't the moment for flipping. It was the moment to consider dropping a nuclear bomb on Afghanistan—not for any strategic or tactical purpose but for the "very strong demonstration effect" that the explosion was likely to make on the rulers of Iran, Iraq, Syria, Libya, and Lebanon. He thought that altering the terrain of Central Asia might persuade Saddam Hussein to obey the instructions of the United Nations, and when asked by a fellow discussant whether he knew that he was talking about the obliteration of an unknown number of miscellaneous Afghans, Simes observed that the NATO victory in Serbia was not won against the Serbian military "but because we were effective against the Serbian civilian infrastructure."

Once placed within the context of the mythical reality, even the most fantastic notions of omnipotence acquire the semblance of everyday sense, which maybe explains why, during the months after the fall of the Twin Towers, both Osama bin Laden and Vice

President Dick Cheney were hiding in caves. Also why President Bush suddenly seemed a more forceful figure, transported between one day and the next into a more vivid interpretation of events, as certain as the agents of Al Qaeda that the world divided into "the camp of the faithful and the camp of the infidels." The President had come home to Hobbiton in the land of a Tolkien romance, a much happier and more comfortable place to live than the world of death and time. So elsewhere in Washington, grateful politicians found themselves possessed of an answer to every question, the fog of doubt and ambiguity chased into Mirkwood by the sun of transcendence and the sound of bugles. Glad of the chance to describe the contest between good and evil in terms as simpleminded as those cherished by its enemies, the American government was offering a $25 million reward for the death or capture of Osama (an advance of $22.5 million over the price of the fatwa posted on the head of Salman Rushdie by the Ayatollah Khomeini) and the American Council of Trustees and Alumni was handing around a report that brought to mind the rule books discovered in the wreckage of the Taliban's Ministry for the Promotion of Virtue and the Prevention of Vice.

All in all, at least for the time being, not an entirely unsatisfactory set of circumstances from the point of view of the Washington political and intelligence establishments anxious to shore up their authority in the aftermath of a calamity that revealed the magnitude of their stupidity and incompetence. The attack was an attack on American foreign policy, which, for the last thirty years, has allied itself, both at home and abroad, with despotism and the weapons trade, a policy conducted by and for a relatively small cadre of selfish interests unrepresentative of (and unaccountable to) the American people as a whole.

Probably because I'm used to reading the letters to the editor of *Harper's Magazine,* I incline to give the American people credit for a higher quotient of intelligence and a greater store of idealism than their supervisors in Washington think they want or deserve, and I suspect that if given a voice in the arrangement of the nation's foreign affairs they would endorse the policies (similar to those once put forward by Franklin D. Roosevelt) that reflected a concern for human rights, international law, nuclear disarmament, freedom from both the colonial and neocolonial forms of economic monopoly. But the American people don't have a voice at the table, especially not now, not during what the media and the government aggressively promote as "a time of war." On numerous occasions last fall the Justice Department placed the country on high alert against an imminent terrorist attack (if not on the Sears Tower or the Golden Gate Bridge, then somewhere in Las Vegas or Miami); it wasn't that anybody knew how or where to forestall such an attack, but rather that the merchants of never-ending crusade wished to enlarge their arsenals of fear and maintain the credulity of the American public at combat strength. Because the civilian population finds itself drafted into service as the target of opportunity for terrorists armed with asymmetric weapons, we're being asked to believe that we're opposed by Morgoth and the Corsairs of Umbar rather than by an incoherent diaspora of desperate human beings, most of them illiterate and many of them children, reduced to expressing their resentment in the impoverished vocabularies of violence. Best not to see our enemies as they are; better to go quietly into the caves of myth thoughtfully prepared by our news media and our schools, there to find, praise be to Allah, our comfort, our salvation, and our glory.

February 2002

Spoils of War

Perpetual peace is a dream, and not even a beautiful dream, and
War is an integral part of God's ordering of the universe. In
War, man's noblest virtues come into play: courage and
renunciation, fidelity to duty and a readiness for sacrifice that
does not stop short of offering up Life itself. Without War the
world would become swamped in materialism.
—GEN. HELMUTH VON MOLTKE

*I*t's been nearly six months since the destruction of the World
Trade Center, and we still haven't come to the end of listening to people say that the world is forever changed. On and
off the record, whether privately at dinner or blowing through the
trumpets of the media, our leading voices of alarmed opinion (politicians, syndicated columnists, retired generals) agree that America can't go home again and that nothing will ever be the same.
Before September 11 the world was one thing; after September
11, the world is something else. Impossible to depict or describe,
of course, but the transformation so unprecedented and complete
as to require new maps and geopolitical surveys, new sets of emotion and states of mind.

The grave announcements invite an equally grave response, but although I usually can manage a solemn nod or worried frown, I'm never sure that I know what it is that I'm being asked to notice or why I can't find in myself the symptoms of an altered sensibility. Apparently the changes don't apply to the kingdom of day-to-day event. The Enron Corporation dissolves in a bankruptcy almost as spectacular as the collapse of the World Trade Center (a market capitalization of $63 billion reduced in nine months to worthless paper), but nobody pokes around in the rubble for a world-changing paradigm; nor does anybody mention radical theories of aesthetics or startling discoveries in the sciences. No miracles being reported elsewhere in the society, I assume that the important talk about "asymmetric reality" and "multilateral chaos" pertains to "the new kind of war" that President George W. Bush has loosed upon all the world's evildoers. It is Osama bin Laden who has rearranged the universe, Osama and his network of elusive assassins holding for ransom not only the Eiffel Tower, Mount Rushmore, and Buckingham Palace but also the beating heart of Western civilization. Madness stalks the earth, and except for Vice President Dick Cheney, none of us is safe.

But if that is the awful truth that divides the world of September 10 from the world of September 12, I'm at a loss to know why it deserves the name of news. Unless I'm badly mistaken or cruelly misinformed, madness has been stalking the earth ever since an American B-29 dropped an atomic bomb on Hiroshima on the day in August 1945 that Buckminster Fuller marked on his calendar as "the day that humanity started taking its final exam." I was ten years old in 1945, too young to understand the remark even if I'd known that Fuller had said it; by the time I was twenty I'd read enough of the literature to know that a radioactive Armageddon doesn't extend the option of any good places to hide, and ever since the Cuban missile crisis in October of 1962 I've understood that I belong to an endangered species, never more than thirty minutes away from an appointment with extinction.

To be held hostage to the fear of a nuclear weapon brought into Manhattan on a truck doesn't seem to me much different than being held hostage to the fear of a nuclear weapon delivered to the same address by a Soviet submarine seventy miles east of Nantucket. The late Robert Benchley put the proposition about as plainly as it can be put on an examination paper that he failed to pass at Harvard in 1912. Asked to frame the legal dispute over fishing rights on the Grand Banks from both the American and the British points of view, Benchley began his answer by saying that he never understood the American argument, never cared to know where England stood, but that he would like to consider the problem from the points of view of the fish. The statement of purpose introduced a dialogue in which a flounder and a cod take up the question as to whether it is better to be roasted in Liverpool, boiled in Boston, or sautéed in Paris.

In several speeches since September 11, President Bush has insisted that "terrorism is terrorism," its character always and everywhere the same, absolute and indivisible, not subject to extenuating circumstance or further explanation. Presumably he refers to terrorist acts staged by independent theater companies, not to the ones sponsored by nation-states. When wrapped up in the ribbons of patriotic slogan, terrorism becomes a show of diplomatic resolve or a lesson in democracy, the prerogative of governments apportioning its distribution to Cambodian peasants, dissident Soviet intellectuals, Israeli disco dancers, Chechen rebels, Palestinian refugees, Iraqi schoolchildren, Guatemalan coffee trees. Except as a form of terrorism, how else do we describe the doctrine of Mutual Assured Destruction that for the last fifty years has trapped the civilian populations of the earth in nets similar to the one in which Benchley's fish found themselves discussing the finer points of British and French cuisine? The doctrine evolved during the prolonged Cold War with the Soviet Union, the diplomatists on both sides of the Iron Curtain entrusting the peace and prosperity of mankind (also the light of reason and the rule of law) to what was bluntly recognized at summit conferences as "the balance of terror"—you kill anybody here, and we kill everybody there; together we preserve humanity by threatening to obliterate it. Citizens inclined to think the arrangement somehow disquieting or oppressive remained free to discuss the finer points of difference between the Russian and the American flag.

If I can understand why the managers of the state monopoly regard the privatization of terror as unwarranted poaching of their market, as a prospective consumer presented with variant packagings of the product I find the same instruction on the labels.

Fear the unknown, reflect upon the transience of flounders, pay the ransom or the tax bill, pray for deliverance. The message is by no means new. The miraculous births of Fat Man and Little Boy in Los Alamos in 1945 pressed the fire of Heaven into the service of a religion (jury-rigged and hastily revealed) founded on the gospels of extortion. Powers once assigned to God passed into the hands of physicists and the manufacturers of intercontinental ballistic missiles; what had been human became divine, the idols of man's own nuclear invention raised up to stand as both agent and symbol of the Day of Judgment.

Historians still argue about whether the arms race was inevitable; some say that it was not, that if President Harry Truman in 1949 had heeded the advice of some of the wisest and most well-informed men in the country (among them Robert Oppenheimer and James Conant) he wouldn't have ordered the development of the hydrogen bomb, and if that program hadn't gone forward, the Russians might not have felt compelled to build their own towers of hideous strength. The Soviet Union at the end of the Second World War possessed few or none of the assets attributed to it by American intelligence operatives, and Stalin conceivably might have welcomed an excuse to forgo the making of weapons (at a cost that the Communist workers' paradise could ill afford) meant to be seen and not heard.

But if I don't know what was being said in Moscow in 1949, I do know that in Washington the managers of American foreign policy cherished the dream of omnipotence cued to a memorandum that George Kennan in the winter of the preceding year circulated within the State Department:

> We have about 50% of the world's wealth, but only 6.3% of
> its population. . . . In this situation, we cannot fail to be the
> object of envy and resentment. Our real task in the coming
> period is to devise a pattern of relationships which will permit
> us to maintain this position of disparity without positive det-
> riment to our national security. To do so, we will have to dis-
> pense with all sentimentality and day-dreaming. . . .

The preferred patterns of relationship presupposed an American realpolitik strong-mindedly turned away from what Kennan regarded as "unreal objectives such as human rights, the raising of living standards, and democratization"; back home in Washington the interested parties (political, military, and economic) bent willingly to the task of replacing the antiquated American republic, modest in ambition and democratic in spirit, with the glory of a nation-state increasingly grand in scale and luxurious in its taste for hegemony. The imperial project flourished under both Democratic and Republican administrations, and over time it achieved the preferred pattern of relationships that Winston Churchill ascribed to the English government in office in 1904, at the moment when Britain reached its zenith as an empire on which the sun never set:

> [A] party of great vested interests, banded together in a for-
> midable confederation, corruption at home, aggression to

cover it up abroad . . . sentiment by the bucketful, patriotism by the imperial pint, the open hand at the public ex-
chequer, the open door at the public-house, dear food for
the millions, cheap labour for the millionaire.

Fattened on the seed of open-handed military spending ($17
trillion since 1950) and grazing in the pastures of easy credit and
certain profit, the confederation of vested interests that President
Eisenhower once identified as "the military-industrial complex"
brought forth an armed colossus the likes of which the world had
never seen—weapons of every conceivable caliber and size, 2 million men under arms on five continents and eight seas and oceans,
a vast armada of naval vessels, light and heavy aircraft, command
vehicles and communications satellites, guidance systems as infal-
lible as the Pope, tracking devices blessed with the judgment of
a recording angel.

The rich displays of armament bear comparison to religious
statuary. No matter what the specific function of the weapons, as
attack submarines or high-altitude gun platforms, they stand as
symbols representative of the divinity (absolute, unfathomable,
unseen but always present) implicit in the cloud of nuclear unknowing. For as long as I can remember I've heard debriefing
officers in Washington say that the end of the world is near at
hand, and I've been told to prepare for "the year of maximum
danger" in 1954, 1962, 1968, 1974, 1983, and 1991. Possibly
because the sounding of the final trumpet has been so often postponed, I no longer take the gentlemen at their word. The Navy
lieutenant stands in front of a lovingly illuminated map overlay,

pointing with an elongated baton to fleets and regiments and force
levels, and I remember that the wealth and worldly power of the
medieval Catholic Church depended upon its cornering of the
market in terror. The lieutenant taps his pointer lightly on a cres-
cent of aircraft carriers or a delicately shaded square of parachute
brigades, and I think of the Jesuit art historian, soft-footed and
subtle, who once conducted me on a tour of the Vatican, directing
my attention to jeweled boxes and silver altarpieces, to ivory
crosses inlaid with gold and lapis lazuli.

  Critics of the military establishment tend to divide into two
camps, those who object to the cost of its maintenance and
those who complain of its incompetence. Neither caucus lacks
reasons for its unhappiness, one of them classifying as extravagant waste the $200 billion contract awarded as recently as last
October to Lockheed Martin for 3,000 F-35 Joint Strike Fight-
ers, the second of them mentioning the loss of the war in Vietnam, the failure to rescue the Shah's Iran or conquer Saddam
Hussein's Iraq. True enough and no doubt sad to say, but the
critics allied with both the liberal and conservative schools of
opinion usually manage to miss the point, failing to appreciate
the military establishment's dual nature as successful business
enterprise and reformed church. How well or how poorly the
combined services perform their combat missions matters less
than their capacity to generate cash and to sustain the images of
omnipotence. Wars, whether won or lost, and the rumors of
war, whether true or false, increase the budget allocations, stim-
ulate the economy, clear the weapons inventory, and add to the

stockpile of fear that guarantees a steady demand for security and promotes a decent respect for authority.

The country has been more or less continuously at war for sixty years, and we can't leave home without it. Otherwise we might not remember that we're the good guys or what would be playing at the movies. During the prosperous decade of the 1990s, the American public showed disturbing signs of weakness, too many people forgetting that without war they were apt to get lost in General von Moltke's "swamps of materialism." The breaking down of the Berlin Wall had brought an end to the skirmish with the Russians, the stock market was going nowhere but up, and the louche example being set by President Clinton in the White House (overweight, emotionally indulgent, morally slack) was bad for children and the weapons business. It wasn't that the American people no longer approved the uses of terrorism as a means of astute crisis-management (in romantic Baghdad or picturesque Kosovo) or as a form of light entertainment (as video game, newspaper headline, and Hollywood plot device), but they had gotten into the habit of thinking that it was a product made exclusively for export.

At Washington policy conferences two and three years before the attack on the Pentagon and the World Trade Center, at least three of the four experts seated on the dais could be counted upon to say that nothing good would come of the American future unless and until the American people awakened to the fact that the world was a far more dangerous place than was dreamed of in the philosophy of Jerry Seinfeld and the World Wildlife Fund. I haven't spoken to any of the panelists since September 11, but I wouldn't be surprised to hear them say that although the attacks were abominable, a criminal outrage, and certainly a lot more destructive than might reasonably have been expected, sometimes people needed harsh reminders to recall them to the banners of noble virtue under which von Moltke's German army invaded Belgium in 1914 and massacred every man, woman, and child in the city of Dinant.

As for the critics who complain that President Bush has been sending ambiguous signals to the American people, once again I think they miss the point. They see a contradiction in the fact that one day he appears on television to say that we confront a future darkened by scenes of unimaginable horror and then, at the next day's press conference, tells everybody not to worry, to remain calm but stay alert, to keep up the strength of their buying in the nearest retail outlet.

Understood as a religious instead of a secular form of communication, the ritual makes liturgical sense. The President first ascends to the pulpit in the persona of the grim but righteous prophet, setting before the congregation a fiery vision of Hell, and then, in the bright sunlight on the steps of the church, he appears as the amiable vicar bidding his flock a kindly and reassuring farewell. Between the sermon and the benediction, a choir of media voices sings the Te Deum, and men in uniform pass the collection plate.

March 2002

The Road to Babylon

> Misgovernment is of four kinds, often in combination.
> They are: 1) tyranny or oppression, of which history provides so
> many well-known examples that they do not need citing;
> 2) excessive ambition, such as Athens' attempted conquest of
> Sicily in the Peloponnesian War, Philip II's of England via
> the Armada, Germany's twice-attempted rule of Europe by a
> self-conceived master race, Japan's bid for an empire of Asia;
> 3) incompetence or decadence, as in the case of the late Roman
> empire, the last Romanovs and the last imperial dynasty of China;
> and finally 4) folly or perversity.
> —BARBARA W. TUCHMAN

When President George W. Bush in his January State of the Union address pronounced the sentence of doom on Saddam Hussein ("America will do what is necessary to ensure our nation's security. . . . I will not wait on events, while dangers gather"), I assumed that he was striking at a target of rhetorical convenience. The war on terrorism was not going as well as planned (Osama bin Laden still at large, Afghanistan not yet transformed into a Connecticut suburb, bombs exploding every seven or eight days on a bus in Israel), and who better than the tyrant of Baghdad to stand surrogate for all the world's evildoers? The man was undoubtedly a villain, a brutal psychopath who murdered children and poisoned village wells, stored biological weapons in hospitals, subjected his enemies to unspeakable torture, and imprisoned his friends in the cages of perpetual fear. Not a nice fellow. Who would not be glad to learn that he had retired from politics or died in a traffic accident? If Mr. Bush chose to express his disapproval in what he called "the language of right and wrong," who was I to deny him his demagogue's right to issue harebrained threats?

The opinion was not widely shared in New York among people possessed of an historical memory (i.e., by individuals who remembered the CIA's staging of "the glorious march to Havana" in the spring of 1961, or the "light at the end of the tunnel" so often seen by General William C. Westmoreland in the forests of Vietnam), but I held to it throughout the spring and early summer even as Mr. Bush mounted the flag-draped rostra at West Point and the Virginia Military Institute to threaten with the vengeance of Heaven far-off men of "mad ambitions," declaring null and void "the Cold War doctrines of deterrence and containment," championing the cause of preemptive action," "forward-looking and resolute." When asked by worried friends and acquaintances whether the President was borrowing his geopolitical theory from the diaries of Joseph Stalin and Adolf Hitler, I assured them that the President didn't have the patience to read more than two or three pages of a Tom Clancy novel. True, the National Security Council was staffed by think-tank ideologues, and yes, some of the policy analysts strolling through the corridors of the White House imagined themselves wearing the uniform of the Bengal Lancers, but no, not even the Bush Administration was so stupid as to take up arms against a figment of its own imagination.

By the second week in August I understood that my assumptions were poorly placed. The spectacle of the American government making preparations for an invasion of Iraq suggested that maybe the Bush Administration was, in fact, stupid enough to call down air strikes on the last four paragraphs of one of the Pentagon's apocalyptic briefing papers. The President was hopping boldly out of golf carts in Texas and Maine to tell the traveling White House press corps that "regime change" was coming soon to downtown Baghdad; in appreciation of the President's enthusiasm and by way of reinforcing his credibility, the Defense Department was supplying the newspapers with documents supposedly top secret that sketched out tactical solutions to the problem of blitzkrieg (the advantages of a simultaneous attack from three directions balanced against the surprise of a swift commando raid, requisitions for 300,000 troops compared to those for only 80,000, something grandiloquent and imperial along the lines of the Japanese attack on Pearl Harbor as opposed to something stylish and postmodern with parachutes, two divisions of light infantry, and a diffusion of Turkish auxiliaries). Senator Joseph Biden (D., Del.), chairman of the Senate Foreign Relations Committee, told a television news camera on August 4 that "there probably will be a war with Iraq. The only question is, is it alone, is it with others, and how long and how costly will it be?" On August 9 a delegation of Iraqi malcontents arrived in Washington to pledge their support of any overthrow of Saddam Hussein that the U.S. Army cared to pay for and arrange. Vice President Dick Cheney spoke to them by video conference from a mountain in Wyoming, reaffirming America's commitment to the principle of regime removal, and Donald Rumsfeld, the secretary of defense, bucked up their spirits with the smiling hope of freedom not far over the military horizon: "Wouldn't it be a wonderful thing if Iraq were similar to Afghanistan, if a bad regime was thrown out, people were liberated, food could come in, borders could be opened, repression could stop, prisons could be opened? I mean, it would be fabulous."

Fabulous for whom? The secretary didn't say; presumably he wasn't referring to the many thousands of people (American soldiers as well as Iraqi civilians) unlucky enough to be killed during the festivities, but none of the Washington correspondents asked why Afghanistan was such a wonderful tourist destination, or when and how it had come to pass that the bandits precariously enthroned in the palace at Kabul exemplified the goodness of free and democratic government. Nor did anybody spoil the upbeat mood of the secretary's press conference with moral or legal questions. Against every precedent in international law, in violation of the United Nations Charter, and without consent of the American Congress, the Bush Administration was proposing to sack a heathen city that had done it no demonstrable harm, and the news media were by and large happy to welcome the event with obedient commentary supportive of the belief that if America allowed Saddam to acquire weapons of mass destruction we would suffer consequences frightful to contemplate and terrible to behold. The lead editorial in *The Economist* on August 3 summed up the consensus of leading opinion in two sentences: "The honest choices now are to give up and give in, or to remove Mr. Hussein before he gets his bomb. Painful as it is, our vote is for war."

Give up to whom? Give in to what? The government didn't stoop to answer simpleminded questions; neither did the grand viziers of the print and broadcast media, who preferred to discuss the complexities of the logistics rather than the purpose of a policy apparently directed at nothing else except the fear of the future, that always dark and dangerous place, where, in five years or maybe ten, something bad is bound to happen. Competing television networks scheduled different time slots for the Pentagon's forthcoming fireworks display—before and after November's congressional election, in early January when the weather around Baghdad improved, next April because the Air Force needed six months to replenish its inventory of precision bombs. Competing newspaper columnists advanced competing adjectives to characterize the "extreme danger" presented to "the entire civilized world," but none of them offered evidence proving that Saddam possessed weapons likely to harm anybody who didn't happen to be living in Iraq; important military authorities appeared on the Sunday-morning talk shows to endorse policies of "forward deterrence" and "anticipatory self-defense," but none of them could think of a good reason why Saddam would make the mistake of attacking the United States; the Senate Foreign Relations Committee on July 31 and August 1 conducted hearings on the question of Iraq and learned that its expert witnesses couldn't say for certain whether they knew what they were talking about. The few shards of undisputed fact collected over two days of testimony suggested that Saddam doesn't sponsor Al Qaeda (or any of the other terrorist brigades that have asked him for money and explosives over the last eleven years), that the Iraqi army, never formidable, is less dangerous now than when it was routed in the four days of the Gulf War, the Iraqi Air Force of no consequence, the civilian economy too impoverished to support the reconstruction of the nuclear-weapons program dismantled by UNSCOM between 1991 and 1998, and Saddam himself best understood as a small-time thug apt to deploy chemical or biological weapons (if he possesses chemical or biological weapons) only as a last and cowardly defense of his own person.

A government that must hold Senate hearings to discover whether it has a reason to go to war is a government that doesn't know the meaning of war. The inanity of the circumstance accounted for the mock-heroic tone of President Bush's golf-cart commuiqués ("I call upon all nations to do everything they can to stop these terrorist killers. Thank you. Now watch this drive") as well as for the sublime complacence of the innumerable spokesmen testifying to the certainties of America's virtue, truth, justice, and power. Consistent with the latter set of assumptions, two of the statements presented to Senator Biden's committee invite lengthy quotation because they speak to the character of a government in the state of decadence. Thus, the heroics of Lieutenant General Thomas McInerney (retired), former assistant vice chief of staff of the U.S. Air Force:

Thank you for this special opportunity to discuss a war of liberation to remove Saddam's regime from Iraq.

I will not dwell on the merits of why he should be removed. Suffice it to say we must preempt threats such as those posed by Saddam Hussein. . . .

I will now focus on the way to do it very expeditiously and with minimum loss of life in both the coalition forces, the Iraqi military and people themselves, and at the same time maintain a relatively small footprint in the region. . . . Our immediate objective will be the following: help Iraqi people liberate Iraq and remove Saddam Hussein and his regime, eliminate weapons of mass destruction and production facilities, complete military operations as soon as possible, protect economic infrastructure targets, identify and terminate terrorism connections, establish an interim government as soon as possible. Our longer term objectives will be to bring a democratic government to Iraq using our post-World War II experiences with Germany, Japan and Italy that will influence the region significantly.

Now I would like to broadly discuss the combined campaign to achieve these objectives using what I will call blitz warfare to simplify the discussion. Blitz warfare is an intensive 24-hour, seven days a week precision air-centric campaign supported by fast moving ground forces composed of a mixture of heavy, light, airborne, amphibious, special, covert operations working with opposition forces that all use effects-based base operations for their target set and correlate their timing of forces for a devastating violent impact. . . .

Using the Global Strike Task Force and Naval Strike Forces composed of over 1,000 land- and sea-based aircraft plus a wide array of air and sea launch Cruise missiles, this will be the most massive precision air campaign in history, achieving rapid dominance in the first 72 hours of combat. . . . [A]ll the Iraqi military forces will be told through the opposition forces in our information operations campaign that they have two choices: either help us change regime leadership and build the democracy, or be destroyed. In addition, commanders and men in weapons of mass destruction forces will be told that they will be tried as war criminals if they use their weapons against coalition forces or other nations.

I can understand the general being sensitive to the question of who is, and who is not, a war criminal. On the same day that he was fitting the First Amendment principle of free speech to the requirement of his information operations campaign (help us build democracy or be destroyed), the United States was demanding immunity from any and all judgments of the International Criminal Court that might find American soldiers guilty of crimes against humanity, which, given the collateral damage soon to be inflicted on the civilian population of Iraq, was a precaution both necessary and wise.

Other points in the general's testimony didn't seem as nicely judged. How does it happen that the "most massive precision air campaign in history" leaves but "a relatively small footprint in the region"? Even if one discounts the devastation of Baghdad as

a minor and scarcely noticeable loss, what is to prevent the con-
flagration likely to erupt in the nearby countries of Saudi Arabia,
Syria, and Iran once the U.S. Air Force has lit up the entire Muslim world with the purifying fires of civil and religious war? Who
prevents Ariel Sharon from upgrading with nuclear weapons the
Israeli program of "preemptive assassination," and, in the relatively
sizable footprint of an oil price marked up to $50 or $70 a barrel,
what happens to the economies of London, Paris, and New York?

The general revealed his plan for waste removal on the first
day of the committee hearings, and on the second day Caspar
Weinberger, a secretary of defense during the Reagan Administration, matched the general's notion of swift military victory in
the desert with an equally fatuous theory of instant political re-
habilitation. Observing that in Washington it was always easy to
find excuses for inaction, Weinberger reminded the senators of
the miraculous American descent on the Caribbean island of Grenada in April 1983:

> We went into Grenada with more troops than everybody
> thought we needed. And we had a very successful operation.
> And prevented the kidnapping and detention of American
> students. And we got out. And we got out in something
> under a month. And a couple of months after that, there
> was a free election. And we have not been back.

Not having kept up with events on Grenada, I have no reason
to doubt Weinberger's happy news, and I'm sure that if Fidel
Castro were to send another invisible flotilla of gunboats, the U.S.

Navy would defend the island against another invisible horde of savage Marxists. Elsewhere in the world, the record of American diplomatic achievement over the last thirty years doesn't inspire a similar degree of confidence. We're good with slogans, but we don't have much talent for fostering the construction of exemplary democracies; we tend to betray our allies, dishonor our treaties, and avoid the waging of difficult or extensive wars. Count through the list of foreign adventures since our hurried departure from Vietnam in April 1975, and we proceed, in random and unseemly sequence, to the exit from Iran and the flight from Lebanon, the pointless assault on Panama, the shutting down of the Gulf War without decisive victory, the abandonment of the Kurds in northern Iraq, the escape from Somalia, the refusal to intrude upon the killing in Rwanda or the Balkans. Drawn to despots whom we hire to represent our freedom-loving commercial interests (Diem, the Shah of Shahs, Somoza, Thieu, Marcos, Jonas Savimbi, Noriega, Saddam Hussein, King Fahd, Arafat, Mobutu Sese Seko, Ariel Sharon), we pretend that our new ally stands as a pillar of democracy in one or another of the world's poorer latitudes, and for however many years the arrangement lasts we send F-16's and messages of humanitarian concern. But then something goes amiss with the band music or the tin mines; the despot's palace guard doesn't know how to fire the machine guns, or fires them at the wrong people, and the prime minister's brother appropriates the traffic in cocaine. We decide that our virtue has been compromised, or that we no longer can afford the cost of the parliament, and we leave by helicopter from the roof of the embassy. The incoherence of our current policy in the Middle East (Saudi Arabia perceived by the Pentagon as our mortal enemy and by the White House as our dearest friend, President Bush committed on Tuesday to the establishment of a Palestinian state, on Thursday to the everlasting kingdom of Zion) suggests that the Washington travel agents have begun considering various estimated times of departure on the assumption that if we can run another "very successful operation" in and out "in something under a month," maybe Oliver North can get everybody to the roof of an embassy to watch the free election.

Fortunately for the republic, both Lieutenant General McInerney and Mr. Weinberger have retired from government service; not so fortunately, they retain the habit of mind that has guided the making of American diplomatic and military policy for the last thirty years. As stupefied as Dick Cheney or Donald Rumsfeld by the romance of imperial power, they speak from within a dream as old as the walls of Troy, and watching them bestow the favor of their prophecies on the Senate committee (to divine Saddam's plans, Senator Biden had said, "is like reading the entrails of goats"), it occurred to me that maybe the time had come to reread Thucydides' *History of the Peloponnesian War*. Much of the story I'd long forgotten, but I remembered that Athens corrupted its democracy and brought about the ruin of its empire by foolishly attempting the conquest of Sicily, and when I found the relevant chapters (the debate in the Athenian assembly prior to sending a fleet westward into the Ionian Sea), it was as if I were reading the front page of that morning's *New York Times*.

Athens in the winter of 415 B.C. stands alone as the preeminent hegemon of Greece. Sparta for the moment has lost its appetite for war, and the Athenians wish to extend their sovereignty over what was then the whole of the known world, not only as far as Sicily but also beyond Carthage to the Pillars of Hercules. Sophists sit around in the wrestling schools sketching with sticks in the sand the map of the Libyan coastline; old men in wine shops babble of victories promised by Egyptian oracles. Ambassadors arrive from Sicily in late March with news of trouble and a request for military assistance. The city of Syracuse threatens to seize the Athenian colony of Segesta, and how can the heirs of noble Pericles stomach so brazen an insult to their pride? What if the Syracusans took it into their heads to attack the glory of Athens?

Uproar and loud shouts of defiance. The impetuous Alcibiades presents the case for "forward deterrence" and "anticipatory self-defense," saying that it is in the nature of Athens to do great deeds. As certain as Lieutenant General McInerney of the city's military power, he assures the assembly that Syracuse is easy prey, weak and badly governed.

> One does not only defend oneself against a superior power when one is attacked; one takes measures in advance to prevent the attack materializing. And it is not possible for us to calculate, like housekeepers, exactly how much empire we want to have.

More uproar. Louder shouts of defiance. The Athenians know as little about Sicily as Senator Biden knows about Iraq ("For the most part ignorant of the size of the island and of the numbers of its inhabitants," says Thucydides, "they did not realize that they were taking on a war of almost the same magnitude as their war against the Peloponnesians"), but they are not the kind of men who stoop to count a crowd of mere barbarians.

Prudent Nicias thinks the Athenians too reckless in their enthusiasm. Like Alcibiades a general, but older and not as eager in his ambition, Nicias raises doubts similar to the ones released in the newspapers during the third week of August by several senior Republican statesmen (among them House Majority Leader Dick Armey and Brent Scowcroft, a former national security adviser) clearly worried both by President Bush's simplistic notions of geopolitics and by the absence of allies, either Arab or European, willing to join the American march on Baghdad. They employed a modern vocabulary, but the substance of their advice they could have borrowed from the speech that Thucydides assigns to Nicias:

> In going to Sicily you are leaving many enemies behind you, and you apparently want to make new ones there and have them also on your hands. . . . [E]ven if we did conquer the Sicilians, there are so many of them and they live so far off that it would be very difficult to govern them. It is senseless to go against people who, even if conquered, could not be controlled, while failure would leave us much worse off than we were before we made the attempt. . . . [T]he next best thing is to make a demonstration of our power and then, after a short time, go away again. We all know that what is

most admired is what is farthest off and least liable to have its reputation put to the test. . . . The right thing is that we should spend our new gains at home and on ourselves instead of on these exiles who are begging for assistance and whose interest it is to tell lies and make us believe them, who have nothing to contribute themselves except speeches, who leave all the danger to others and, if they are successful, will not be properly grateful, while if they fall in any way they will involve their friends in their own ruin.

The argument fails to make an impression. So excessive is the enthusiasm of the majority, says Thucydides, "that the few who actually were opposed to the expedition were afraid of being thought unpatriotic if they voted against it, and therefore kept quiet." The assembly declares for war, and over the next several months Athens musters an invasion fleet conforming to the current Pentagon doctrine of "overwhelming force" (134 triremes, expensively gilded; impressive numbers of archers, slingers, and javelin throwers; merchant vessels stocked with soothsayers and cavalry horses), and on a sunny day in July 415 B.C., trumpets blow, priests pour wine into golden bowls, and "by far the most costly and splendid" expedition "even sent out by a single city" sails to its appointment with destruction.

During the last weeks of August 2002, it was hard to miss the newspaper reports of a splendid and costly American force gathering in the Middle East—merchant vessels putting to sea loaded with armored vehicles, helicopters, large stores of ammunition; the air base at Qatar upgraded with a runway convenient to heavy bombers and equipped with tents capable of housing 3,800 troops; a premium of $2 a barrel added to the price of Arabian oil to meet any sudden shift of supply or demand. Speaking to a battery of press cameras in Crawford, Texas, President Bush said that yes, he was aware of questions about the wisdom of invading Iraq (the doubts expressed both by members of his own party and, increasingly, in various alarmed sectors of the national news media), and yes, he would "listen very carefully" to what other people had to say, but no, he didn't think it necessary to complicate the decision with too much extraneous discussion. "America needs to know," he said, "I'll be making up my mind based upon the latest intelligence and how best to protect our own country plus our friends and allies."

Unwilling to expose "the latest intelligence" to the vulgar, democratic light of day, the President reserves the right to do what he, and he alone ("forward-looking and resolute," as brave as Alcibiades, disinclined to "wait on events, while dangers gather"), deems just. Taken together with the proven incompetence of the American intelligence agencies and the delusions of military grandeur cherished by the secretary of defense, the President's belated assurance that he would "continue to consult" ("When I say I'm a patient man, I mean I'm a patient man . . .") sounded both grudging and false. He had been shaking the fist of war at Iraq for two years, talking up the prospect of "regime change" to audiences both foreign and domestic, and how could the noble heir to the throne of Teddy Roosevelt retreat from his promise of retribution frightful to contemplate and terrible to behold?

The question was framed not by the President himself but by several Washington operatives closely allied with the administration and currently serving on the Pentagon's Defense Review Board. James Schlesinger, former secretary of defense, spoke for the jingoist majority: "Given all we have said as a leading world power about the necessity of regime change in Iraq means that our credibility would be badly damaged if that regime change did not take place."

The ancient Greeks at least had a prize in view—the harbors of Sicily and the wealth of Carthage; the Bush Administration erases the distinction between the reasons of state and the uses of publicity, and if we invade Iraq apparently we'll be doing so to make credible the President's boyish and theatrical saber-rattling with a blurb from the U.S. Air Force.

As a form of misgovernment that satisfies all the definitions set forth at the head of this essay in the epigraph borrowed from Barbara Tuchman's book *The March of Folly*, I can think of none more disastrous than the failure to distinguish fiction from fact, to substitute for the waging of war the making of war movies. Mark Twain remarked on the stupidity in 1905 during the American occupation of the Philippines. Objecting to the fraudulent piety of statesmen who don't know what they're saying, Twain wrote a story, "The War Prayer," in which an "aged stranger" enters a church where the congregation has been listening to an heroic sermon about the glory to be won in battle by young patriots armed with the love of God. Motioning the startled minister to stand aside, the aged stranger improvises a bitter peroration that makes clear the true meaning of the prayer:

O Lord our God, help us to tear their soldiers to bloody shreds with our shells; help us to cover their smiling fields with the pale forms of their patriot dead; help us to drown the thunder of the guns with the shrieks of their wounded, writhing in pain; help us to lay waste their humble homes with a hurricane of fire; help us to wring the hearts of their unoffending widows with unavailing grief; help us to turn them out roofless with their little children to wander unfriended the wastes of their desolated land in rags and hunger and thirst, sports of the sun flames of summer and the icy winds of winter, broken in spirit, worn with travail, imploring Thee for the refuge of the grave and denied it— for our sakes who adore Thee, Lord, blast their hopes, blight their lives, protract their bitter pilgrimage, make heavy their steps, water their way with their tears, stain the white snow with the blood of their wounded feet! We ask it, in the spirit of love, of Him Who is the Source of Love, and Who is the ever-faithful refuge and friend of all that are sore beset and seek His aid with humble and contrite hearts. Amen.

The story didn't see the light of print until 1923, thirteen years after Twain's death. The editors to whom he tendered the manuscript thought it "unsuitable" for publication at a moment of high and patriotic feeling.

October 2002

Hail Caesar!

> Allow the President to invade a neighboring nation whenever he
> shall deem it necessary to repel an invasion . . . and you allow
> him to make war at pleasure. . . . If today he should choose to
> say he thinks it necessary to invade Canada to prevent the
> British from invading us, how could you stop him? You may say
> to him, "I see no probability of the British invading us," but he
> would say to you, "Be silent: I see it if you don't."
> —ABRAHAM LINCOLN

A fter the pretense of a debate that lasted less than a week, Congress on October 11 invested President George W. Bush with the power to order an American invasion of Iraq whenever it occurred to him to do so, for whatever reason he might deem glorious or convenient. Akin to the ancient Roman practice of enthroning a dictator at moments of severe crisis, the joint resolution was hurried into law by servile majorities in both a Senate (77–23) and a House of Representatives (296–133) much relieved to escape the chore—tiresome, unpopular, time-consuming, poorly paid—of republican self-government. The sergeants-at-arms didn't take the trouble to dress up the occasion

with a slaughter of sacrificial sheep or the presentation of a bull
to Apollo, but the subtext of the vote could be understood as a
submissive prayer:

> Our President is a Great General; he will blast Saddam Hus-
> sein and rescue us from doom. To achieve this extraordinary
> mission he needs extraordinary powers, so extraordinary that
> they don't exist in law. The barbarians are at the gates, but
> our general is all-knowing, and he sees what we cannot.
> Great is Caesar; God must be with him.

I don't know whether Diane Sawyer appeared on camera to
release a fluttering of doves, but the prophets in the temples of
the institutional news media didn't forget the business with the
mirrors and the smoke. Following the scripts pre-positioned by
the White House and the Pentagon, the chorus of solemn editorial
voices interpreted the policy of preemptive bombing, precision-
guided and courteously brief, as a form of compassionate conservatism. It wasn't that America would go willingly to war, but
neither could it allow the forces of nuclear darkness to gather in
the palaces of Baghdad. War was never easy and not to be lightly
undertaken, but catastrophe loomed on both the far and near ho-
rizons, and who could doubt that Saddam must be destroyed? Not
Citigroup or ExxonMobil; not the *New York Times*, CBS, the
Washington Post, NBC, the *Wall Street Journal*, Fox News, or *USA
Today*.

A few objections showed up on the margins of consensus—in
political journals of modest circulation, on the Saturday op-ed

pages and National Public Radio, among a scattering of guests on cable television—but none of them were loud enough to disabuse the parade marshals in Washington of their fond assumption that the votes in Congress fairly represented the electorate's faith in God's will and Caesar's sword.

The news analysts cited the corroborating testimony of the opinion polls—a 70 percent approval rating for President Bush, 60 percent in favor of sending the army to exterminate Saddam— but in New York during the months of September and October I could find little trace or sign of the militant spirit presumably eager to pat the dog of war. Not once in six weeks did I come across anybody who thought that the President had made a co- herent argument in favor of an invasion of Iraq. Whether at lunch with film producers in Greenwich Village or at dinner among investment bankers over-looking Central Park, the com- mentary on the President's repeated attempts at explanation in- variably descended into sarcasm. Who could take seriously the reasoning of a man armed with so few facts—no proof of Sad- dam's connection to Al Qaeda, no indication that Iraq threatens the United States (or even the nearby states of Jordan, Saudi Ara- bia, and Iran), no evidence that Saddam possesses weapons of mass destruction, the presidential indictment based on surveil- lance photographs too secret to be seen, on old stories of past atrocities and the premise that America "did not ask for this present challenge, but we accept it"?

The last statement, drawn from the President's speech in Cin- cinnati on October 7, prompted a civil rights lawyer the next morning at breakfast to mockery. "To whom does the man think he's talking?" she said. "To people so stupid that they can't see through the window of his lies? A Republican administration promotes a foreign war to hide the mess of its domestic politics, and the President asks us to believe that we're being attacked by Joseph Stalin?"

The lady voiced a New York opinion, and I accepted it as such. Given my long confinement in the city's spheres of literary influence, I don't know many people who admire President Bush or who feel anything but loathing for the reactionary scholars who teach him lessons in geography. In New York I expect to hear Bush compared to Little Lord Fauntleroy or Bernie Ebbers, and I take it for granted that nearly everybody else in the conversation shares my own low regard for the corporate-management theory that informs the making of American foreign policy.

What I didn't expect was the fierce opposition to the Iraqi adventure that I encountered elsewhere in the country. Traveling in California in September and October, and then in Oregon, Connecticut, and Virginia, I sought out fellow citizens unmarked by the stigmata of effete, liberal intellectualism—an aerospace engineer on the plane to Portland, a quorum of computer programmers in Hartford, two retired admirals on a golf course in San Diego, various unpublished social critics met with in hotel coffee shops and airport bars. It was as if I hadn't left New York. Never once did I find myself in the company of people who approved the Pentagon's strategies of "forward deterrence" and "anticipatory self-defense." The general opinion of President Bush wavered between the phrases "toy soldier" and "dangerous fool." A woman in San Francisco, a lifelong Republican who once had run a campaign headquarters for Governor Ronald Reagan, wondered whether the President had become stupefied by his desire for revenge. "I hear him say of Saddam that 'he tried to kill my Dad,' and I start to think that maybe I learn more about the White House from *The Sopranos* than from *The West Wing*." The aerospace engineer observed that many of the allegations brought against Saddam (possession of nuclear weapons, harboring terrorists, etc.) also could be charged to the account of the United States. "If we preemptively bomb other countries whenever we think we smell a rat," he said, "how can we not expect an increase in both the number and the violence of the attacks on us? Scrap the hope of international law, and all you've got left is the old news that might makes right; the strong do as they please, the weak do as they're told. Wonderful for military contractors; not so good for everybody else."

The more senior of the two admirals made a similar point. As a student of both the Spanish and the Austro-Hungarian empires, he had noticed that warrior kings invariably impoverish their people while pretending concern for their safety, and on the tee at the twelfth hole he remembered a maxim that had been impressed upon him at the Naval War College by a lecturer quoting the historian A.J.P. Taylor: "Though the object of being a Great Power is to be able to fight a Great War, the only way of remaining a Great Power is not to fight one."

Other voices in the wilderness asked questions that seldom make their way past the velvet rope at ABC News or the headwaiters at *Time* magazine—"Why must the security of every other nation in the world be subordinated to the comfort of the United

States?" "I thought we learned from our mistake in Vietnam that we're no good at the mechanics of regime change?" "If Bush means what he says about a war on terrorism, why doesn't he begin by disarming the Arab and Israeli terrorists in Jerusalem and the Gaza Strip?"

Neither the candor nor the intelligence of the discussions beyond the perimeter of Washington reached the floor of what the media falsely advertised as the "debate" in Congress. "Appearance of debate" would have come closer to the mark, a theme-park performance, paltry in its substance, unctuous and condescending in its tone. A few forthright speeches proved exceptions to the rule of cowardice, and I was glad of the chance to hear Nancy Pelosi (D., Calif.) in the House as well as Robert Byrd (D., W.Va.) in the Senate. Pelosi counted the costs to the American economy of an unnecessary war waged to pay the bill for the administration's incompetent diplomacy; Byrd declaimed against both the ignoble scurrying to dispose of the question of Iraq ("Haste is blind and improvident, Mr. President, blind and improvident") and the betrayal of the Constitution ("What a shame. Fie upon the Congress"), and it was among his remarks that I found the apposite quotation at the head of this essay, Lincoln in 1848 writing a letter to William Herndon to explain his opposition to the Mexican war.

Most of what else I could hear or read of the speechmaking on Capitol Hill consisted of threadbare propaganda or rank hypocrisy. The time taken up with quibbling over the syntax and punctuation of the "Authorization for the Use of Military Force Against Iraq" rescued all present from the embarrassment of having to talk about the abdication of their legislative authority to the whim of a lying President. Nobody questioned the corruption of language that elevated random acts of criminal violence to the declaration of World War III; nor did anybody concede the brutal truth that no power on earth—not the CIA, the United States Marines, the Department of Homeland Security; not God or Yale or Caesar—can hold the United States harmless against the risk or fear of death.

Instead of arguing with one another, the politicians read prepared statements into the C-SPAN cameras, striking handsome poses, producing certificates of their moral character and worth, expressing their "deep concern" for human suffering and their "profound awareness" of the distinction between war and peace, before bowing to the knee of circumstance and to what for six months they had known would prove to be the will of the majority.

The question is why. Why the lack of courage on the part of our elected representatives, and why the hurry, as Tom Daschle, the Senate majority leader, put it on *Meet the Press* on October 6, "to move on"? Move on to where? President Bush had served Congress with notice of its irrelevance, and who would want to annoy the man by making a rude noise? Not Senator Daschle, not any loyal and patriotic public servant glad to escape the unpleasantness of speaking truth to power. Better to move on, quietly and as soon as possible, to a campaign rally in South Dakota, where a senator could count on a show of respect (also a round of

applause and an apple pie) from voters grateful for a defense contract, a farm subsidy, or a dam.

The Sunday-morning talk shows rounded up the usual suspects
to provide the usual set of dismal answers as to why so many
prominent Democrats (among them Senators Hillary Clinton,
John Kerry, and Diane Feinstein) deserted both the army of their
constituents and the flags of their convictions—the polls showing
strong flows of patriotic sentiment, the Republicans suborned by
the White House and the Democrats worried about the position-
ing of their images in the autumn election campaigns, political
partisanship feckless and unseemly in a time of trouble, the President in need of loud congressional support in order to extort an
effectively punitive resolution from the U.N. Security Council.

Few or none of the assertions could match the weight of the
follow-up questions. If the poll results published under the newspaper headline on page one showed 60 percent of the respondents
supporting an invasion of Iraq, the further analysis of the numbers
continued on page thirty-four showed the support to be tentative
and ambivalent—37 percent unless the invasion was undertaken
at the behest of the United Nations and in concert with numerous
allies; not even a bare majority persuaded that Saddam presents a
more imminent threat to the United States than the agents of Al
Qaeda, 40 percent believing that President Bush's rush to war
follows from motives having less to do with the security of the
United States than with the security of his administration's hold
on power—i.e., a shell game not unlike the one with which Saddam entertains the people of Iraq.

Nor did the voters seem to be in a mood to punish displays of principle or conscience. During the three days after his speech to Congress Senator Byrd received more than 50,000 letters and emails approving of what he'd said, also 18,000 telephone calls; demonstrations protesting a war in Iraq made their way onto college campuses and into Central Park (25,000 people assembled on the East Meadow on October 6).

If the Sunday talk show wisdom didn't answer to the facts, why then the silence of the lambs? Possibly because the Congress represents the constituency of the frightened rich—not the will or the spirit of what was once a democratic republic but the interest of a scared and selfish oligarchy anxious to preserve its comforts in the impregnable vaults of military empire. The grotesque maldistribution of the country's wealth over the last thirty years has brought forth a class system fully outfitted with the traditional accessories of complacence, stupidity, and pride. People supported by incomes of $10 or $15 million a year not only mount a different style of living than those available to an income of $50,000 or even $150,000 a year, they acquire different habits of mind— reluctant to think for themselves, afraid of the future, careful to expatriate their profits in offshore tax havens, disinclined to trust a new hairdresser or a new idea, grateful for the security of gated residential protectorates, reassured by reactionary political theorists who say that history is at an end and that if events should threaten to prove otherwise (angry mobs rising in Third World slums to beg a chance at freedom or demand a piece of the action) America will send an army to exterminate the brutes.

Not an inspiring set of attitudes, but representative of the social class that owns our news media, staffs the White House, and pays for our elections. If neither the Republicans nor the Democrats have stumbled upon a forceful or generous political idea since 1968, it's because the widening distance between the American citizenry and the American elites obliges the candidates of both parties to go for money to the same body of comfortable opinion (the few hundred thousand individuals, interest groups, or corporations that contribute more than $1,000 to any one campaign) content to think that the idealism implicit in what Benjamin Franklin recognized as the American experiment has run its course, served its purpose, gone far enough. Whether sporting lapel pins in the shape of elephants or donkeys, the members of Congress dance to the tune of the same big but nervous money, the differences in their political views reduced to a choice between the grilled or potted shrimp.

It's conceivable that we might soon see a change in the program. The American citizenry isn't as dumb as the American elites condescendingly like to think and believe, and if it can be generally understood that an ill-conceived war with Iraq comes to us courtesy of the same feeble-mindedness that set up the Enron and WorldCom swindles, we might learn to elect politicians who speak to our courage and intelligence rather than to our weakness and fear.

December 2002

Regime Change

They that can give up essential liberty to obtain a little
temporary safety deserve neither liberty nor safety.
— BENJAMIN FRANKLIN

*U*nrelenting in its search for Osama bin Laden and the
roots of all the world's evil, the Defense Department
some months ago established an Information Awareness
Office that took for its letterhead emblem the all-seeing eye of
God. Although still in the early stages of development and for
the moment funded with an annual budget of only $200 million,
the new medium of mass investigation seeks to "detect and classify" every prospective terrorist (foreign, hybrid, mutant, or native
born) setting foot on American soil. No door or envelope un-
opened, no secret unexposed, no suspicious suitcase or Guatemalan
allowed to descend unnoticed from a cruise ship or a bicycle.

To give weight and form to a paranoid dream of reason not
unlike the one that sustained the sixteenth-century Spanish In-

quisition, the government apparently means to recruit a synod of high-speed computers capable of sifting through "ultra-large" data warehouses stocked with every electronic proof of human movement in the wilderness of cyberspace—bank, medical, and divorce records, credit-card transactions, emails (interoffice and extraterritorial), college transcripts, surveillance photographs (from cameras in hospitals and shopping malls as well as from those in airports and hotel bars), driver's licenses and passport applications, bookstore purchases, website visits, and traffic violations. Connect all the names and places to all the dates and times, and once the systems become fully operational, in four years or maybe ten, the protectors of the public health and safety hope to reach beyond "truth maintenance" and "biologically inspired algorithms for agent control" to the construction of "FutureMap"—i.e., a set of indices programmed into the fiberoptic equivalent of a crystal ball that modifies "market-based techniques for avoiding surprise" in such a way that next week's nuclear explosion can be seen as clearly as last week's pornographic movie. In the meantime, while waiting for the technical upgrades with which to perform "entity extraction from natural language text," the clerks seated at the computer screens can look for inspiration to the mandala on their office stationery—an obverse of the Great Seal of the United States similar to the ornament on the back of the $1 bill, an Egyptian pyramid and mystic, Rosicrucian light buttressed by the tendering in Latin of the motto "Knowledge is power."

When reports of the IAO's existence belatedly appeared in the mainstream press in November of last year, nine months after the headquarters' staff began moving the first electronic robots into

an air-conditioned basement in Virginia, the news didn't capture
the attention of the Congress or excite the interest of the television
networks. No politician uttered a discouraging word; no prominent historian entertained the risk of a possibly unpatriotic question. The talk-show gossip of the moment dwelled on the prospect
of war in Iraq and the setting up of the Department of Homeland
Security (soon to be equipped with its own domestic espionage
service), and except for an occasional lawyer associated with the
American Civil Liberties Union, most of the people in New York
to whom I mentioned the Pentagon's gift for totalitarian fantasy
were inclined to think that intelligence gathering was somehow
akin to weather forecasting—a routine and necessary precaution,
annoying and possibly unconstitutional but entirely appropriate
in a time of trouble.

William Safire entered an objection on the opinion page of *The
New York Times* ("Orwellian scenario . . . sweeping theft of privacy
rights . . . exploitation of fear"), but elsewhere in the large-
circulation media protests were hard to find. The general opinion
so clearly favored the Bush Administration's policies of forward
deterrence and preemptive strike that I wasn't surprised by the
absence of commentary, much less complaint, when it was announced in early December that the FBI had been jettisoning the
baggage of due process while pursuing the rumor of an underwater
attack against an unknown target somewhere along the 95,000
miles of the American coastline. From hundreds of dive-shop op-
erators everywhere in the country the FBI demanded the names
of the several million swimmers who had taken diving lessons over
the course of the last three years. Only two citizens refused the

request, the co-owners of Reef Seekers Dive Company in Beverly Hills, California. When word of their noncooperation showed up in a newspaper story, they were besieged by vindictive telephone calls expressing the hope that their shop prove to be the next locus of a terrorist bombing.

The incident speaks to the nervous temper of the times—hundreds of dive shops, only one refusing to give up its client list; the voice of the people tuned to the pitch of an angry mob—and illustrates the lesson in obedience well and truly learned by a once free people during the second half of a century defined in the history books as America's own. I'm old enough to remember public speeches unfettered by the dogma of political correctness, a time when it was possible to apply for a job without submitting to a blood or urine test, when people construed their freedoms as a constitutional birthright, not as favors grudgingly bestowed by a sometimes benevolent government. I also can remember the days when people weren't afraid of tobacco smoke, sexual intercourse, and saturated fats; when irony was understood and money wasn't sacred; when even men in uniform could be trusted to recognize a joke.

The spacious and once familiar atmospheres of liberty (wisecracking and open-ended, tolerant, unkempt, experimental, and democratic) didn't survive the poisoning of Hiroshima or serve the purposes of the Cold War with the Russians. The easygoing, provincial republic of fifty years ago gradually assumed the character of a world-encircling nation-state, its plow shares beaten into swords, borrowing from its enemies (first the nonexistent Communist empire, now the unseen terrorist jihad) the practice of restricting the freedom of its own citizens in the interest of what the increasingly oligarchic governments in Washington proclaim to be "the national security." Begin the narrative almost anywhere in the late 1940s or early 1950s—with the National Security Act of 1947, the hearings before the House Un-American Activities Committee in 1951, President Harry Truman's decision to build the hydrogen bomb, the composition of the Hollywood Blacklist, or Senator Joe McCarthy's search for Marxists marching in the Rose Bowl Parade—and the plot development moves briskly forward in the direction of more fear and less courage, toward the substitution of White House intrigue for congressional debate and the professions of smiling loyalty preferred to the clumsy and impolitic fumbling for the truth.

Bear in mind the conclusion of the Church committee hearings as long ago as 1976—"too many people have been spied upon by too many Government agencies and too much information has been collected"—and space permits only a brief acknowledgment of the various police powers seized by the government under the rubric of the war on drugs (the use of anonymous informants, the taking of property without conviction or arrest), of the illegal surveillance of American citizens by their own intelligence agencies (the CIA between 1953 and 1973 producing an index of 1.5 million suspicious American names, the FBI compiling a list of 26,000 individuals to be summarily rounded up in the event of "a national emergency"), of the Justice Department's long campaign against the civil liberties expressed in the First, Fourth,

Fifth, Sixth, and Eighth amendments to the Constitution, and of a system of public education that offers its best-attended courses of instruction to the student populations in the army and the prisons. Add to the constant threat of nuclear extinction the sum of the wiretaps infiltrated into the American consciousness across the span of three generations, and it's no wonder that by the late 1990s, even in the midst of the reassuring prosperity allied with a buoyant stock market, and well before the destruction of the World Trade Center, the public-opinion polls found the bulk of the respondents willing to give up a generous percentage of their essential liberty in return for safer streets, secure suburbs, well-lighted parking garages, and risk-free cocktail waitresses.

Since the shock of September 11, 2001, the American public has quickened the pace of its retreat into the shelters of harmless speech and heavy law enforcement. If I were to measure the general level of submissiveness by my own encounters with the habit of self-censorship and the general concern with social hygiene—acquaintances reluctant to remark on the brutality of the Israeli army for fear of being thought anti-Semitic, public scolds who damn me as a terrorist for smoking a cigarette in Central Park, college students so worried about the grooming of their résumés that they avoid rock concerts on the off-chance that their faces might show up on a police-department videotape—I might be tempted to argue that America's winning of the Cold War resulted in the loss of its soul. In place of the reckless and independent-minded individual once thought to embody the national stereo-type (child of nature, descendant of Daniel Boone, hard-drinking and unorthodox) we now have a quorum of nervous careerists, psalm-singing and well-behaved, happy to oblige, eager to please, trained to hold up their hands and empty their pockets when passing through airport security or entering City Hall.

John Quincy Adams understood the terms of the bargain as long ago as 1821, speaking as the secretary of state against sending the U.S. Navy to rearrange Spain's colonial empire in Colombia and Chile. America, he said, "goes not abroad, in search of monsters to destroy." Were the country to embark on such a foolish adventure,

> she would involve herself beyond the power of extrication, in all the wars of interest and intrigue, of individual avarice, envy, and ambition, which assume the colors and usurp the standard of freedom. The fundamental maxims of her policy would insensibly change from liberty to force. . . . She might become the dictatress of the world. She would no longer be the ruler of her own spirit.

The Bush Administration equates the American spirit with power, not with liberty. During the months since the fall of the twin towers it has assumed the colors and usurped the standard of freedom to jury-rig the framework of an autocratic state. If not as a concerted effort to restrict the liberties of the American people, how else does one describe the Republican agenda now in motion in the nation's capital? Backed by the specious promise of imminent economic recovery and secured by the guarantee of never-ending war, the legislative measures mobilized by the White House and the Congress suggest that what the Bush Administration has in mind is not the defense of the American citizenry against a foreign enemy but the protection of the American oligarchy from the American democracy. In every instance, and no matter what the issue immediately at hand, the bias is the same— more laws limiting the rights of individuals, fewer laws restraining the rights of property:

1. The systematic transfer of the nation's wealth from the union of the poor to the confederacy of the rich. President Bush's new plan to exclude from taxation all corporate dividends received by individuals, at the same time lowering the income-tax rates previously scheduled to take effect between now and 2009, assigns the bulk of the refund (64 percent) to the wealthiest 5 percent of the nation's taxpayers, more than half of the award to people earning at least $200,000 a year, a quarter of it to people earning more than $1 million a year.

2. The easing of environmental regulations on the energy industries in New England.

3. The opening of the national forests in the Pacific Northwest and the Arctic National Wildlife Refuge to further expropriation by the oil, gas, mining, and timber industries.

4. The persistent issuing of health-insurance regulations intended to subvert and eventually overturn the 1973 Supreme Court ruling, *Roe v. Wade*, that recognized a woman's freedom to decide whether or not she will give birth to a child.

5. The reinforcing of the monopolies held by the big media syndicates on the country's systems of communication.

6. Outfitting the banks and credit-card agencies with the privilege to sell to the highest bidders any or all of the personal data acquired from their customers.

7. A series of bills in Congress meant to reduce the nation's health-care costs by denying medical services to people too poor to pay for the upkeep of the insurance companies.

8. The nomination to the federal appeals courts of judges apt to find legal precedents in the Bible rather than in the Constitution.

9. The broad expansion of the government's police power and the Justice Department's reserving to itself the right to tap anybody's phone and open everybody's mail, to decide who is and who is not an un-American.

The Homeland Security Act runs to a length of 484 pages, and when it was presented to Congress last November Senator Robert C. Byrd of West Virginia flung the text down on his desk with a gesture that reminded a *New York Times* reporter of "the fury of Moses smashing the tablets." One of only nine senators who voted against the bill, Byrd denounced it as a foolish and unlawful seizure of power unlikely to do much harm to America's enemies but certain to do a great deal of harm to the American people. "With a battle plan like the Bush Administration is proposing," Byrd said, "instead of crossing the Delaware River to capture the Hessian soldiers on Christmas day, George Washington would have stayed on his side of the river and built a bureaucracy."

Not having read the small print in the Homeland Security Act, I can't guess at the extent to which it will further subtract from the country's store of civil liberty, but if I understand correctly its operative bias (170,000 functionaries undefended by a labor union and serving at the pleasure and sole discretion of the president of the United States), I all too easily can imagine a new department of bureaucratic control that incorporates the paranoid systems of thought engendered by the Cold War with the dogmas of political correctness meant to cure the habit of free speech, and deploys the surveillance techniques made possible by the miracles of modern telecommunications technology.

I don't count myself a believer in the dystopian futures imagined in Aldous Huxley's *Brave New World* or George Orwell's *1984*, but I think it would be a mistake to regard the trend of events as somehow favorable to the cause of liberty. President Bush likes to present himself as the embodiment of the spirit of 1776, but to the directorship of the Pentagon's new Information Awareness Office he appointed Vice Admiral John Poindexter, a royalist ideologue, a convicted felon, and a proven enemy of both the

American Congress and the articles of the Constitution. As national security adviser to President Ronald Reagan in 1985, the admiral supervised what came to be known as the Iran-Contra swindle—the selling of missiles to the despotic ayatollahs in Iran in return for money with which to fund, secretly and illegally, a thuggish junta in Nicaragua. After the scheme collapsed under the weight of its criminal stupidity, the admiral repeatedly lied to the congressional committee investigating the farce (thus his convictions on five felony counts), and when called upon to account for his false testimony he said that he considered it his "duty" to conceal information too sensitive to be entrusted to loud-mouthed politicians.

Not an honest or liberal-minded man, the admiral, but unfortunately representative of the arrogant corporatists currently in charge of the government in Washington. Glimpsed in the persons of Secretary of Defense Donald Rumsfeld, Vice President Dick Cheney, and Attorney General John Ashcroft, the senior managers of the Bush Administration make no secret of their contempt for the rules of democratic procedure (inefficient, wrong-headed, and slow), their distrust of the American people (indolent and immoral, corrupted by a debased popular culture, undeserving of the truth), and their disdain for the United Nations and the principle of international law (sophomoric idealisms popular with weak nations too poor to pay for a serious Air Force). I don't for a moment doubt the eager commitment to the great and noble project of "regime change," but on the evidence of the last eighteen months they've been doing their most effective work in the United States, not in Afghanistan, Saudi Arabia, or Iraq. Better understood as radical nationalists than as principled conservatives, they borrow the logic endorsed by the American military commanders in Vietnam (who found it necessary to destroy a village in order to save it), and they offer the American people a choice similar to the one presented by the officers of the Spanish Inquisition to independent-minded heretics—give up your liberty, and we will set you free.

February 2003

Cause for Dissent

> The dissenter is every human being at those moments
> of his life when he resigns momentarily from the herd
> and thinks for himself.
> —ARCHIBALD MACLEISH

As a director of the government's ministry of propaganda during World War II, Archibald MacLeish knew that dissent seldom walks on stage to the sound of warm and welcoming applause. As a poet and later the librarian of Congress, he also knew that liberty has ambitious enemies, and that the survival of the American democracy depends less on the size of its armies than on the capacity of its individual citizens to rely, if only momentarily, on the strength of their own thought. Unpopular during even the happiest of stock-market booms, in time of war the voices of objection attract the attention of the police. The parade marshals regard any wandering away from the line of march as unpatriotic and disloyal; the unlicensed forms of speech come to be confused with treason and registered as crimes, and in the skyboxes of the news media august personages reaffirm America's long-standing alliance with God and the Statue of Liberty. Counting through the list of the country's exemplary virtues—a just cause, an invincible air force, a noble truth—they find no reasons for dissent. On the threshold of a war in Iraq, I can think of nine.

I. AGITPROP

Whether expressed in the language of religious exorcism by President Bush in his annual message to Congress or chopped into nourishing sound bites by National Security Adviser Condoleezza Rice for the fans of CNN's *Larry King Live*, the government's brief for a prompt and bloody regime change in Baghdad rests on the principle announced nearly a year ago by Secretary of Defense Donald Rumsfeld at a press conference in Brussels. Asked by a crowd of European journalists for proof of the assertion that weapons of mass destruction confronted the United States with a clear and present danger, Rumsfeld said, "The absence of evidence is not evidence of absence."

Secretary of State Colin Powell didn't come up with a substantially different explanation in early February when he presented the United Nations Security Council with a slide show meant to serve as a trailer for the forthcoming action movie soon to be filmed in the deserts of Iraq. The surveillance photographs of Iraqi trucks demanded the kind of arcane exposition that New York art critics attach to exhibitions of abstract painting. By way of adding drama to the performance, Powell held up a vial of white powder (meant to be seen as anthrax but probably closer in its chemistry to granulated sugar) and rolled tape of two satellite telephone intercepts of Iraqi military officers screaming at one another in Arabic, but he didn't provide an answer to the question, Why does America attack Iraq when Iraq hasn't attacked America? In lieu of demonstrable provocations Mr. Powell offered disturbing signs and evil portents, and when the voice of Osama bin Laden turned up a week later on an audiotape broadcast from Qatar, the secretary seized upon the occasion to discover a "partnership" between Al Qaeda and the government of Iraq. No such conclusion could be drawn from even a careless reading of the transcript, but to Mr. Powell the sending of a message (any message) proved that Osama bin Laden and Saddam Hussein somehow had morphed into the same enemy.

The secretary's power points didn't add to the sum of a convincing argument, but then neither did the advertising copy for the Spanish-American War or the sales promotions for the war in Vietnam, and if the agitprop failed to persuade the French, Russian, or Chinese representatives to the Security Council, it was more than good enough for the emissaries from the major American news media. Our television networks and large-circulation newspapers trade in the same commodity. They identify themselves as instruments of the American government rather than as witnesses beholden to the American people, and they bring to their work the talents and the haircuts of expensive corporate lobbyists. In Secretary Powell's remarks to the U.N. the editors of the *Wall Street Journal* discovered echoes of Talleyrand and Metternich.

2. THE KOREAN EXCEPTION

The Bush Administration makes a boast of its "moral clarity" and principled resolve, also of its willingness to "exercise power without conquest" and "sacrifice for the liberty of strangers." Why then no imbecile invasion of North Korea?

Although cold in the winter, the country abounds in unfortunate strangers, and unlike the reports being brought back to New York in February by Hans Blix and International Atomic Energy Agency director general Mohamed ElBaradei the news from Pyongyang that month amounted to something more than a threatening hypothesis. A Communist despotism controlled by a heartless dictator easily the peer of Saddam Hussein had resumed its manufacture of enriched uranium and expelled the U.N. inspectors assigned to monitor its Yongbyon nuclear reactor complex. Three bombs were thought to exist, several others were said to be within a few months of production; the civilian population had been reduced to near starvation, and the army, believed to number a million soldiers, heavily armed and fanatic in its devotion to "the Dear Leader," was stationed within artillery range of the 30,000 American troops just south of the demilitarized zone. The North Korean threat was both plainly visible and alarmingly present, but it was not one against which the United States cared to launch the wrath of its aircraft carriers. Confronted with Kim Jong-il's blunt demand for ransom money (payment acceptable in trade agreements, bank credit, or bags of rice), the Bush Administration referred the unpleasantness to the United Nations—the same United Nations that Secretary Rumsfeld had deemed "irresponsible" and on "a path of ridicule" because of its reluctance to endorse an American expedition to Baghdad. The referral dimmed the lamp of moral clarity, and the cautious retreat to the policy of containment that President Bush had declared obsolete drew the distinction between threats both real and apparent and those cleverly hidden by illusory enemies who also happen to command small armies and govern countries rich with oil.

3. "WE REFUSE TO LIVE IN FEAR."

President Bush presented the statement to an audience in Cincinnati on October 7, and of all lies told by the government's faith healers and gun salesmen, I know of none as cowardly. Where else does the Bush Administration ask the American people to live except in fear? On what other ground does it justify its deconstruction of the nation's civil liberties?

Ever since the September 11 attacks on New York and Washington, no week has passed in which the government has failed to issue warnings of a sequel. Sometimes it's the director of the FBI, sometimes the attorney general or an unnamed source in the CIA or the Department of Homeland Security, but always it's the same message: suspect your neighbor and watch the sky; buy duct tape, avoid the Washington Monument, hide the children.

Let too many citizens begin to ask impertinent questions about the shambles of the federal budget or the disappearance of a forest in Montana and the government sends another law-enforcement officer to a microphone with a story about a missing tube of plutonium or a newly discovered nerve gas.

4. SOMNAMBULISM

Washington these days suffers no shortage of visionary geopoliticians touting the wonders of an American empire imposing, by
act of conscience and force of arms, peace on earth and good will
toward men. The prophets enjoy the patronage of power, some of
them White House privy counselors, others advisers to the Pentagon, all of them utopian anarchists. They envision a slum-
clearance project for the whole of the Islamic Middle East, Iraq
the first in a series of model democracies soon to be erected in
Syria, Iran, Libya, Egypt, and Saudi Arabia, and when reading
their articles in the policy journals, I remember a remark I once
came across in a novelist's description of four Marxist assassins
seated at a café table in Paris in the 1920s: "They believe everything they can prove, and they can prove everything they believe."

The Bush Administration employs a good many ideologues af-
flicted with a similarly messianic turn of mind and who take for
granted the stupefaction of an electorate too lazy to open its mail.
Assuming a general state of political somnambulism not much
different from their own, the authors of the government's press
releases count on an audience that thinks of politics as trivial
entertainment. The supposition isn't entirely wrong.

The successful operation of a democracy relies on acts of government by no means easy to perform, and for the last twenty
years we have been unwilling to do the work. Choosing to believe
that the public good comes to us at the discretion of private
wealth, all politicians therefore as interchangeable as hotel bar-
tenders, we don't bother to vote, don't read through the list of

budget appropriations, content ourselves with the opinions advertised on prime-time television by talk-show guests holding up
little vials of important news—sometimes anthrax, usually sugar.
Our prosperity finances the habits of indolence. We leave the small
print for the lawyers to clean and maybe press, and in place of an
energetic politics we get by with nostalgic sentiment and the
public-spirited postcards sent by PBS—elections a cascade of balloons, liberty a trust fund, and America the land in which the
money never dies.

5. THE INSOLENCE OF OFFICE

In a recent and best-selling book, *Bush at War*, Bob Woodward
presents a portrait of the president so flattering that had it been
rendered in oil on canvas, the curator of the White House art
collection might wish to hang it in the Blue Room. One of the
bons mots that Woodward attributes to his subject could as easily
have been attributed to Louis XIV: "That's the interesting thing
about being the President. Maybe somebody needs to explain to
me why they say something, but I don't feel like I owe anybody
an explanation."

The administration's senior ministers share the view. Often pet-
ulant and openly contemptuous of opinions not their own, they
listen to opposing argument with impatience and disdain. At the
United Nations last winter, when the French and German statesmen raised pointed questions about both the necessity and the
timing of a police raid on Iraq, Mr. Rumsfeld received the skep-
ticism as an insult. France and Germany, he said, spoke for an

"old Europe" long ago reduced to a harmless tourist attraction, France a country famous for its vanity and pride; Germany stubborn and wrongheaded.

At the higher altitudes of Washington officialdom, the tone of condescension is traditional. Dean Acheson, secretary of state in the Truman Administration, understood as long ago as 1947 that if America wished to do as it pleased in the world, it would be necessary to come up with a slogan that could serve as both a reason and an explanation for high-handed, unilateral decision. Knowing that the American people might balk at the prospect of the Cold War if they thought the strategy open to discussion, Acheson explained to his associates in the State Department that the country's foreign policy must be presented as "nonpartisan," that any and all political argument "stops at the water's edge."

"If we can make them believe that," Acheson said, "we're off to the races."

Over the next two generations the word "nonpartisan" proved invaluable to a succession of presidents bent on waging declared and undeclared wars in Korea, Vietnam, Guatemala, Grenada, Panama, Cambodia, Lebanon, Nicaragua, Angola, and the Persian Gulf. Replace the once magic word "nonpartisan" with the phrase "never-ending war on terrorism," and we arrive at the policy of Rumsfeld the Implacable and the wisdom of Cheney the Unseen.

6. NEGLIGENCE

The destruction of the World Trade Center evoked an immense surge of pro-American feeling everywhere in the world—in Cairo and Amman as well as in London and Paris. Within the brief span of nineteen months our government has managed to squander al-most the whole of the asset. Mocked by its failure to find Osama bin Laden, the Bush Administration has bullied our allies, scorned the United Nations, subverted the principle of international law, recruited an angry host of new enemies, and exchanged the hard currency of our inherent idealism for the counterfeit coin of a hare-brained cynicism.

In return for what? A "regime change" in Afghanistan. The horse-drawn and all but helpless Taliban put to rout at a cost of more than $15 billion, Kabul remanded to the custody of a freedom-loving warlord, and tranquillity along the border of Pak-istan achieved with a $250 million bribe paid to the military dictatorship of General Pervez Musharraf.

7. OUR STAUNCHEST ALLY

When I look at the handsome maps with which the Pentagon marks out the road to glory in Iraq, I'm sure that I miss a good many of the military fine points, but I never doubt that the maps must gladden the heart of Osama bin Laden. Who but Osama stands to pluck so rich a prize from the fires of holy crusade? Fresh recruits for Al Qaeda, the Western democracies at odds with one another (and their intelligence agencies therefore less cooperative), the scourge of civil war conceivably spread across the whole of the Middle East, the Saudi Arabian monarchy maybe overthrown, and Israel possibly forced onto the reefs of destruction.

As utopian an anarchist as the Washington apostles of Amer-ican empire, Osama preaches a parallel vision of a world trans-formed, justice restored, and the desert cleansed of its impurities.

President Bush knows that the work of pious destruction is blessed by the God of Abraham and that liberty is the gift of heaven and not the work of men. Allah the all-merciful sends Osama an American army bringing the torches and the mops.

8. BARBED WIRE

Unable to erect a secure perimeter around the life and landscape of a free society, the government bureaus of public safety solve the technical problems by seeing to it that the society becomes less free. The USA Patriot Act has been reinforced so many times since it was first passed by Congress in October 2001 that by now the country's law-enforcement agencies have been equipped with as many powers as they choose to exercise—random search, unwarranted seizure, arbitrary arrest.

Every month brings with it some new proof of the frightened and punitive states of mind that inform the imposition of additional rules, more efficient procedures, further restrictions. My notes from the last week in January through the second week in February mention the dropping of a blue curtain over a tapestry of Pablo Picasso's *Guernica* outside the Security Council chambers (to preserve Secretary Powell from the embarrassment of having to pose for photographs in front of a work of art depicting the horrors of war), Laura Bush canceling a poetry symposium at the White House when told that one or more of the poets might read an antiwar poem, the New York Police Department forbidding an antiwar march in front of the United Nations, a consortium of scientific journals (among them *Nature* and *The New England Journal of Medicine*) agreeing to censor any articles that might compromise national security, and then, most unequivocally, in January the Department of Transportation proposing to establish a system of records classifying any and all commercial airline passengers as suspected terrorists and thus subject to background investigations that might otherwise require a court order.

9. SLOTH

The question most often asked of the American mission to Iraq can be reduced to two words: "Why now?" I've listened to numerous explanations—the weather, America's credibility at stake, Saddam about to poison Israel's reservoirs—but I suspect that the best answer is the simplest. War is easier than peace. The government elects to punish an enemy it perceives as weak because it's easier to send the aircraft carriers to the Persian Gulf than to attempt the harder task of making an American society not so wretchedly defaced by its hungry children, its crowded prisons, and its corporate thieves.

The Bush Administration owes its existence to our apathy and sloth; if we have allowed the American political argument to degenerate into mindless catchphrase and the fifteen-second sound bite, how can we not expect our government to think in the same language, to depend for its authority on the easy and patriotic lie, and whenever it doesn't know what else to do, to arrest mysterious strangers and bomb Iraq?

April 2003

Shock and Awe

> If we go back to the beginning we shall always find that
> ignorance and fear have created gods; fancy, enthusiasm, or
> deceit has adorned or disfigured them; weakness worships them;
> credulity preserves them in life; custom regards them and
> tyranny supports them in order to make the blindness of men
> serve its own ends.
> —BARON D'HOLBACH

*P*rior to the Third Infantry Division's advance into the valley of the Euphrates on March 21, I had occasion this past winter to travel frequently in Europe, twice in December and then again in early January and late February, and from one week to the next, in four countries and five languages, I met with expressions of anti-American feeling that steadily increased in both their intensity and force. The newspapers and television broadcasts never were at a loss for reports of the failing diplomacy at the United Nations, and whether in a Paris restaurant or a London park, on the train from Geneva to Zurich or at a hotel bar in Rome, it didn't matter where or how the conversation began. Once past the preliminary remarks about the traffic and the weather, I could count on the questions turning hostile. Was it the Iraqi oil fields that we wished to seize, or was it the Pentagon, keen to test a new, color-coordinated line of high explosives? Were the Americans serious in their intention to build in the Mesopotamian desert a Potemkin village of democracy? Was the White House policy being guided by the friends of Greater Israel? Did Colin Powell have a mind or principle of his own, or was he some sort of Christmas windup toy placed in front of a government microphone to broadcast prerecorded greetings of humanitarian concern? Was President Bush better understood as a clumsy thief or a pious thug?

The sarcasms fit the profile of the caricature long cherished by the standard-bearers of Europe's finest drawing-room opinion—the Americans seen as brute materialists, hardheaded and pragmatic, good with machinery but culturally illiterate, ferocious in our love of money and famous for our feats of gluttonous consumption, trusting only what we can count or eat, a nation of philistines blind to the distinctions between Beethoven and Molière but certain of the difference between a profit and a loss.

The European wits make the mistake of portraying us as a secular people enslaved to numbers and bound by facts, descendants of the eighteenth-century Enlightenment, loyal in our allegiance to the scientific method and holding fast to Voltaire's "principle of universal reason." The caricature fails to account for the several varieties of American religious experience, and even the British choose not to notice that Jehovah is alive and well and often angry not only in Texas and Tennessee but also in the halls of Congress. Our national opinion polls report 46 percent of the respondents registering themselves—together with President George W. Bush—as evangelical Christians, twice born and therefore safe within the garden of redemption; 48 percent denying as heresy the theory of evolution, another 68 percent knowing that it has met or seen the Devil. More than 50 million readers buy the novels that tout the miracle of the Second Coming and borrow their plotlines from the Babylonian prophecies foretelling the Rapture and the Tribulation. Attorney General John Ashcroft asserts that in the United States "we have no king but Jesus," and Tom DeLay, the Republican majority leader in the House of Representatives, says that he has been assigned by God to promote "a biblical worldview" in American politics, that "only Christianity offers a way to live in response to the realities that we find in this world—only Christianity."

President Bush professes his devotion to the same creed, and when answering questions in London or Paris about the American purpose in Iraq (code name "Shock and Awe"), I usually found it necessary to begin with the distinction between a secular and a religious approach to foreign policy. A European electorate might not possess a thorough knowledge of a particular border or trade dispute, but everybody understands the dealing between nations as a dull and tiresome business, heavy with historical antecedent and unyielding in its financial details, encrusted with the familiar sores of ambiguity, hypocrisy, and spite. As Americans, we look for "moral clarity" and for a shuffling of interests more lively and cinematic—a war to end all wars, Darth Vader or the Angel Moroni hiding somewhere in the mountains, a shooting script complete with uplifting parables and the dialogue in the form of sermons invariably laconic, weather-beaten, barely audible.

It was under the flags of a transcendental diplomacy that the Americans waged war against the Mexicans in the 1840s, the doctrine of Manifest Destiny having revealed to them God's blessing of the horses and the guns. Horace Greeley in 1859 updated the doctrine to accommodate the slaughter of the Plains Indians: "These people must die out—there is no help for them. God has given this earth to those who will subdue and cultivate it, and it is vain to struggle against his righteous decree." President Woodrow Wilson enlisted the country in the first of the twentieth century's world wars under the banner of Christian crusade and took the trouble to write the Fourteen Points that he brought to the Paris Peace Conference in 1919 because "America had the infinite privilege of fulfilling her destiny and saving the world." Then as now, the Europeans were slow to grasp the American connection to divine Providence, and on first reading a draft of Wilson's manifesto, Georges Clemenceau, the French prime minister, looked up from the page and said, "Even the Lord Almighty limited Himself to Ten!"

When President Bush appeared in the White House on the evening of March 6 to announce the imminent scourging of Iraq, it was a wonder that he didn't speak in tongues. His topic was secular, but his message was spiritual, the blank expression engraved on his face disquietingly similar to the thousand-yard stare of the true believer gazing into the mirror of eternity. Answering questions for the better part of an hour from the assembled scribes and pharisees, the president bore witness to a revelation mounted on four pillars of holy wrath:

1. America allies itself with Christ and goes to war to rid the world of evil.

2. Iraq is Sodom, or possibly Gomorrah.

3. Saddam is the Devil's pawn.

4. Any nation that refuses to join the "coalition of the willing" deserves to perish in the deserts of disbelief.

The president knows himself allied with the thrones of Christian virtue, and from the mouths of his biographers the adoring phrases pour forth as if from Solomon's well of living waters, perfumed with myrrh and frankincense: "steely, eye-of-the-storm serenity," "casting his mission and that of the country in the grand vision of God's master plan," "humble leader of a great country," "impervious to doubt," "brother in Christ." Left to his own or his speechwriters' devices in front of an open microphone, the president seldom misses a chance to restate the good news in the language of the Bible:

"The liberty we prize is not America's gift to the world, it is God's gift to humanity."

"We do not claim to know all the ways of Providence, yet we can trust in them, placing our confidence in the loving God behind all of life, and all of history."

"Events aren't moved by blind change and chance . . . [but] by the hand of a just and faithful God."

"The crew of the shuttle *Columbia* did not return safely to earth. Yet we can pray that all are safely home."

"We will export death and violence to the four corners of the earth in defense of our great nation."

I don't doubt that somewhere on a road in Texas or a pond in Maine, the president beheld a great light, but I find as little sense in what he says as I find in the rustling of leaves or the pattering of rain. The failure in translation I attribute to my early education, which was entirely secular in its character and curriculum. On hearing my first Sunday sermon, at the age of thirteen in the white and gold chapel of a New England boarding school, I responded with the firm applause that I'd been taught was owed to a commencement or a campaign speech. Brought up to admire the founders of the American republic as men defined by the energy of their intellect and the courage of their experiments, for the last fifty years I've been content to regard the bows that politicians make to an altar or a cross as a courtesy that reason pays to superstition. The candidate has come in search of votes, and he doesn't wish to slight the native handicrafts or walk in the wrong direction around the totem poles.

President Ronald Reagan's wearing of religion on his sleeve I could understand as a compliment to the choir, but unless I took President Bush at his literal, messianic word, I didn't know how else to explain to various European bystanders how it had come to pass that America meant to fight the battle of Armageddon in Iraq. Because the crowd at the café table invariably assumed that I must be joking, I found myself at some pains to draw the connection between the evangelist's dream of Heaven and the politician's blueprint of Utopia. Both real estate speculations speak to our American wish to believe in what isn't there: Saddam Hussein's store of thermonuclear weapons, the Vietnamese army wading ashore at Waikiki, the perfect orgasm made to order by Christina Aguilera. The foreign observers who deplore the rapaciousness of our appetite for the goods and services of a spendthrift economy miss the point of the enterprise. The material objects serve as testimonials to the desired states of immateriality—not what the money buys but what the money says about our rank and standing in the company of the saved. Eager to behold visions in the wilderness, captivated by the power of metaphor and the promise of transcendence, we're suckers for any sales promotion designed to rescue us from the wreck of time. Our fondness for the immaterial and invisible, for the name of the thing instead of the thing itself, is what sells the sports utility vehicle or the soap; entire vocabularies of meaningless jargon—temporal as well as spiritual, literary, scientific, political, and economic—describe entire kingdoms of nonexistent thought. The most successful prophets of sexual happiness and social transformation discover that the less they know about the subject in question, the more easily they can escape the mortal coil of inconvenient fact and so float effortlessly upward into the spheres of radiant abstraction.

*   *   *

If my revisionist portrait of the true American as a born poet and natural metaphysician wasn't deemed credible in Italy, Switzerland, France, and England, it was because the other people in the room didn't wish to believe that America had come so dangerously loose from its moorings in the eighteenth-century Enlightenment. Their angry objections to our preemptive strike at Iraq followed from a sense of loss and disillusion. What had happened to the story told by Thomas Paine, or to the hope of a democratic republic founded on the laws of nature and the rule of reason? Where was the wisdom of Abraham Lincoln, or the humanitarian idealism of Franklin D. Roosevelt?

The questions don't lend themselves to reassuring answers. The sight of President George Bush shaking the fist of righteousness at the Four Horsemen of the Apocalypse doesn't bring to mind the political theory of James Madison; I think instead of Jonathan Edwards preaching a furious sermon to a congregation of sinners in colonial Massachusetts ("The bow of God's wrath is bent, and the arrow made ready on the string, and justice bends the arrow at your heart . . ."), or possibly of Al-Hajjaj, who assumed the governorship of Baghdad in the year 694, and greeted the inhabitants with a message meant to administer shock and inspire awe: "O people of Iraq . . . by God, I shall strip you like bark, I shall truss you like a bundle of twigs, I shall beat you like stray camels. . . . By God, what I promise, I fulfill; what I purpose, I accomplish; what I measure, I cut off."

*   *   *

The makers of America's liberties were discoverers of new plants and new stars, delighting in what Thomas Jefferson called "the inimitable freedom of the human mind," bringing to their studies of science and philosophy the excitement of explorers mapping the headwaters of the Missouri River or measuring the transit of Venus—Benjamin Franklin (author, printer, inventor, statesman), William Bartram (botanist), Thomas Paine (essayist, engineer), Benjamin Rush (physician, chemist), Thomas Jefferson (author, architect, diplomat, agronomist). They didn't have much use for priests, and they insisted on the separation of church and state, not because they feared the power of the state to harm religion but because they feared, more sensibly, the power of religion to harm the state. Mindful of the religious wars in Europe, of the St. Bartholomew's Day Massacre, the fires of the Catholic Inquisition, and the blood-soaked cross of the medieval Crusades, Jefferson associated the power of religion with a tyranny that "has been severely felt by mankind, and has filled the history of ten or twelve centuries with too many atrocities not to merit a proscription from meddling with government."

Tirelessly curious about all things great and small, the inventors of the American idea pursued what they took to be the proper study of mankind in as many spheres of reference as they could crowd into a Philadelphia library company or a Boston philosophical society, always with the hope of constructing a government on the blueprint of universal reason despite, again in Voltaire's words, "all the passions which struggle against it; despite the tyrants who wish to drown it in blood; despite the imposters who would employ superstition to bring it to naught."

President Bush speaks for an earlier period in American history, from a pulpit in the Puritan forest before it received the gift of books. If his biographers can be trusted, we now have in the White House a president so secure in his belief that the course of human events rests in "the hand of a just and faithful God" that he counts his ignorance as a virtue and regards his lack of curiosity as a sign of moral strength. A similarly primitive way of thinking (fearful, intolerant, fond of magic) darkens the mind of the shamans drawing up the Pentagon's plans for the conquest of evil and accounts for the punitive reign of virtue currently being imposed upon the American body politic by the Justice Department, the Congress, and the Supreme Court. The collective retreat into the mist of a simplified past speaks to the exhaustion of the mentality that framed the Constitution and for two centuries carried forward the American experiment with freedom. Our Washington geopoliticians like to imagine their war on terrorism as "a clash of civilizations." They flatter themselves with the high-toned, plural noun; what they have incompetently in hand is a clash of superstitions, and when I listen to them talk I hear the rattle of feathered drums and the braying of archaic horns.

May 2003

The Demonstration Effect

All you have to do is to tell them that they are being attacked,
and denounce the pacifists for lack of patriotism and exposing
the country to danger. It works the same in every country.
—HERMANN GÖRING

*I*f by Easter Sunday the purification of Iraq was still a work
in progress—Saddam Hussein nowhere to be found, sporadic
gunfire lingering in the streets of Basra and Mosul, a new
government not yet seated on its prayer rugs—in Washington the
flags were blooming on the bandstands, and the heralds of American empire were crying up the news of great and glorious victory.
Our forces under the command of General Tommy Franks had
destroyed the semblance of an Iraqi army, rescued the oil fields of
Kirkuk, chased an evil tyrant from his throne, cleansed the Tigris
Valley of an unsanitary regime. Priced at a cost of $60 billion and
129 American lives (forty-five of them lost in accidents), the
month's work lifted President George W. Bush to a 70 percent
approval rating in the opinion polls, the friends and officers of his

administration everywhere attended by congratulatory nods and the gifts of loyal applause. Important newspaper columnists pointed proudly to the "high-water mark" of America's "resurgent power"; elevated sources at the White House declared themselves well pleased with "the demonstration effect" of a military maneuver that "opens all sorts of new opportunities for us."

As to the nature of the new opportunities and the use of precision-guided bombs as an inspirational sales technique, I don't doubt that over the next few months we can expect the publication of numerous manuals (political, military, and geostrategic) reflecting on the lessons learned in the deserts of Mesopotamia. Because the teaching almost certainly will be expressed in government-inspected prose, I have undertaken to reduce the syllabus to its principal points of interest:

The moral splendor of American empire can be made to stand on a pedestal of lies.

During the months prior to the bombing of Baghdad on March 19, every government spokesman in Washington likened Saddam Hussein to Adolf Hitler or Joseph Stalin, a villain "stifling the world," his powers all but supernatural and thus presenting an immediate and terrible danger not only to the peoples of Saudi Arabia, Israel, and Kuwait but also to every man, woman, and child in the United States. Saddam was said to be hiding nuclear weapons, allied with the terrorist networks of Al Qaeda, and complicit in the events of September 11, plotting monstrous but unspecified attacks (if not tomorrow or next week, then two or four or six months hence), extending the reach of his murderous regime across the whole of Central Asia and the Middle East, certain to oppose any attempts at punishment with vengeful clouds of poison gas.

The first week of invasion proved every assertion false. In place of Hitler or Stalin, the American armies found the remnants of a dictator more accurately compared to a psychopathic prison warden, a brutal but almost comic figure, so enslaved to the dream of his omnipotence that he apparently had trusted the defense of his kingdom to histrionic press releases and gigantic portraits of himself armed with a shotgun and a porkpie hat.

No Iraqi shock troops appeared in the field against the American infantry divisions; no Iraqi aircraft presumed to leave the ground; no allied combat unit met with, much less knew where to find, the fabled weapons of mass destruction. The desultory shows of resistance at the river crossings constituted ragged skirmish lines of young men for the most part barefoot and lightly armed, so many of them out of uniform that it wasn't worth the trouble to distinguish between the civilian and the military dead.

The weakness of the Iraqi target made ridiculous Washington's propaganda poster of Saddam as the second coming of Adolf Hitler, and the useful lesson to be learned presented itself on April Fool's Day. Here was the American army in the sinister landscape of Iraq, equipped to fight the Battle of Normandy or El-Alamein but conducting a police action in the manner of the Israeli assassination teams hunting down Palestinian terrorists in the rubble of the Gaza Strip. Would it be possible to hide in plain sight the false pretext of Operation Iraqi Freedom? The Bush Administration answered the question with its customary mendacious aplomb, simply by changing the mission statement. The American army had not come to Iraq to remove the totalitarian menace threatening all of Western civilization—absolutely not; the American army had come briefly eastward out of Eden to "liberate" the long-suffering Iraqi people from the misery inflicted upon them by an evildoer with the bad habit of cutting out their tongues. One excuse for war was as good as any other.

The American news media can be relied upon to sell the spectacle and leave the story to the government.

The news transmissions from the fog of war were as relentless as the bombing raids on Baghdad: incessant, deafening, blind to the hope of a coherent narrative. The twenty-four-hour montage on the cable channels resembled the dream sequences of a commercial for men's cologne, the misinformation and the disinformation deftly intercut with the frontline first impressions, the images so quickly revised, repeated, updated, cross-promoted, or shifted to another camera angle—mortar rounds entering stage left, an artillery barrage exiting stage right, two- and three-star generals parading to and fro on Tom Brokaw's reviewing stand, the correspondent aboard an aircraft carrier handing the microphone across a split screen to the correspondent in a Bradley fighting vehicle—that before the invasion was two days north of Umm Qasr the accelerated data stream was as impenetrable as the sandstorm descending on the 3rd Infantry Division's auxiliary helicopters.

The demonstration effects multiplied the news media's enthusiasm for their assignment to Camp Adventure, and they did their best to tell a tale worthy of Stephen Ambrose or Rudyard Kipling. Journalists on duty at the Pentagon characterized the assault as a magnificent achievement, one of the most extraordinary military campaigns ever conducted in the history of the world; reporters traveling with the troops discovered comparisons to the glory of World War II—the tanks in the desert reminding them of Generals George Patton and Erwin Rommel, the siege of Basra analogous to the defense of Stalingrad. The hyperbole never quite squared with the discernible facts. Every day's news cycle began with rumors of appalling danger on both the near and far horizon (the Iraqi Republican Guard entrenched in a grove of palm trees, a battalion of Arab martyrs infiltrating the Syrian border, "heavy fighting," "pockets of resistance," etc.), but by the time the reporters reached the scene of rumored slaughter, the proofs of its occurrence were nowhere to be found. A few wrecked or burning trucks, the flashes of a distant explosion, once or twice an Iraqi corpse, but never any American casualties, no Republican Guard, no Arab martyrs or enemy artillery. The media made up the loss of awe-inspiring sights by starting the clock on another news cycle (more to come, don't go away) or by lending ballast to the photo opportunities. The pulling down of Saddam's statue on April 9 achieved parity with the crumbling of the Berlin Wall, even though the event took place in an all-but-empty plaza cordoned off by a perimeter of U.S. Marines, in the presence of maybe 150 pro-American Iraqis, half of them imported by the Pentagon several days earlier from London. The careful framing of the camera shots sustained the illusion of an immense and wildly cheering crowd.

When temporarily short of footage incoming from Iraq, the television networks in Washington and New York dressed up their screens with American flags and courageous anchorpersons pledging allegiance to "America's Bravest." MSNBC decorated its primary set with a portrait of President Bush—the studio equivalent of a loyalty oath. Erik Sorenson, the executive in charge of the network, was proud to say that the press had no business asking ugly or discourteous questions. "After September 11 the country wants more optimism and benefit of the doubt. . . . It's about being positive as opposed to being negative."

At Fox News the talking heads transformed their jingoistic fervor into an article of totalitarian faith, speaking directly to any scoundrels who might have wandered into the viewing audience with the dissenting notion that the war was not a war and therefore unnecessary as well as wrong—"You were sickening then, you are sickening now," "leftist stooges," "absolutely committing sedition, or treason." The *New York Times* added a further proof of the media's subservience to the government when, on April 21, one of its reporters filed a dispatch (dictated by American army officers and before publication submitted to their approval) announcing the discovery of Saddam's illegal chemical weapons by an unnamed Iraqi scientist, seen at an unspecified distance, wearing a baseball cap and pointing to an unknown object buried in the sand. The reporter wasn't allowed to speak to the man, but the paper printed her account on page one, below a headline suggesting that the Bush Administration finally had found the long sought and much hoped for casus belli of its splendid little war.

Package the imperialist agenda as instructive entertainment, and the American public will come to know and love the product.

The fireworks display over old, romantic Baghdad inspired heroic feats of merchandising not only on the part of the Pentagon and White House briefing officers but also among the manufacturers of cigars and women's underwear. The excitement prompted a flurry of applications for the trademark "Shock and Awe"; together with the cigars and women's underwear the list of products included teddy bears, bubble-making wands, doll-house furnishings, ski boots, mouse pads, smoking jackets, yo-yos, and inflatable bathtub toys.

Concerns about the possible squeamishness of the prime-time audience when exposed to scenes of horror proved to be unwarranted and overblown. The computer animations of the weapons systems and the tactical movements looked like video games, the "virtual views" of the topography like the golf-course graphics deployed to illustrate the perils of the PGA Tour.

On the first day of hostilities President Bush cautioned the country's senior news executives against publishing photographs of dead Iraqi civilians. As events moved forward and the home audience registered its approval of a new and improved form of reality TV, it was understood that foreign dead counted merely as unpaid extras briefly available to the producers of the nightly news to stand around in front of the machine-gun bullets and fuel

the fireballs. By April 12 the American public had shown sufficient bravery in the face of a foreign enemy that the *New York
Times* didn't think it imprudent to publish a handsome color photograph of dead Iraqi children thrown like spoiled vegetables into
a refrigerated truck.

But if the pictures didn't present a problem, one still had to
be careful with the words. As a matter of well-known and long-
established principle, imperialist powers shoot and kill only for
the good of the people shot down, but the policy usually requires
some sort of upbeat euphemism ("the training of backward peoples" in the art of "democratic self-government," the building of
a "free and flourishing" Sumatra or Iraq) with which to ease the
minds of the women and children in the room. The producers of
The March on Baghdad took the necessary precautions. The killing of Iraqis, both military and civilian, was softened to "attriting"
or "degrading" resources; when it was noticed that in Arabic the
word "Fedayeen" means "one who sacrifices himself for a cause,"
our official spokesmen substituted "terrorist death squads"; the
looting of the Iraqi National Museum and the burning of the
country's National Library were ascribed to the joys of "freedom."
Nothing to do with our Navy's cruise missiles, of course, and in
no way the fault of our Army units that had been asked to protect
both buildings, and with them the 12,000-year history of a civilization that prior to the arrival of General Franks had survived
the conquests of the Emperor Heraclius, Suleiman the Magnificent, and Genghis Khan. Secretary of Defense Donald Rumsfeld
scowled at the suggestion that somehow the destruction could
have been prevented, possibly in the same way that American

troops preserved the Oil Ministry. "Freedom's untidy," he said, "and free people are free to make mistakes and commit crimes and do bad things."

So are military empires free to seize "all sorts of new opportunities" opened to them by "demonstration effects" similar to the ones brought by an Athenian army to the island of Melos in the summer of 416 B.C. Having first butchered the Melian military commanders, the Athenians presented the citizens of the town with the choice of abandoning their loyalty to Sparta or accepting the sentence of death.

"As practical men," said the Athenian heralds, "you know and we know that the question of justice arises only between parties equal in strength, and the strong do what they can, and the weak submit."

The corporate managers of the Bush Administration lack the concision of the Attic style, but they didn't find it hard to appreciate the ancient moral of the tale. The high-tech gladiatorial show in the Iraqi coliseum had served as a test market not only for the Pentagon's new and exciting inventory of weapons but also for the premise of American military empire—set the proper tone, established the necessary precedent, opened the road to the grandeur that was Rome. The absence of objection on the part of the American public and the American news media suggested that the truth didn't matter, that motive was irrelevant, that the Bush Administration was free to do as it pleased.

Heartened by the message not likely to be lost on either the voters in next year's presidential election or America's enemies both east and west of Suez, various staff officers attached to the

White House, its supporting neo-conservative think tanks, and the Pentagon expressed varying degrees of satisfaction. Secretary of State Colin Powell threatened Syria, telling a press conference that Syria would have to change its ways, but, no, "no war plan right now." Vice President Dick Cheney admonished Germany and France, indicating that neither country could expect oil or construction contracts from a new jurisdiction in Iraq, saying that "perhaps, time will help in terms of improving their outlook."

Ken Adelman, a member of the Pentagon's Defense Policy Board, hoped that the conquest of Baghdad "emboldens leaders to drastic, not measured, approaches," but it was left to Michael Ledeen, resident scholar in the Freedom Chair at the American Enterprise Institute, to place the great victory in its clearest perspective. "Every ten years or so, the United States needs to pick up some crappy little country and throw it against the wall, just to show the world we mean business."

Welcome to the brave, new freedom-loving world envisioned by the heirs and assigns of what was once a democratic republic. Let any nation anywhere on earth even begin to think of challenging the American supremacy (military, cultural, socioeconomic), and America reserves the right to strangle the impudence at birth—to bomb the peasants or the palace, block the flows of oil or bank credit, change the linen in the information ministries and the hotels.

June 2003

Index